"How could it have happened?"

Fifteen-year-old Tammy sat across from me in our small Bible study group. Her face was white and her voice trembled as she spoke. "I found out when I got to school yesterday. Rick killed himself. He shot himself. I couldn't believe it. Just like that. And no one seems to know why."

She kept looking at her hands folded on her lap. "I saw him just the day before in school. I keep asking myself: 'Could I have said something — done something to stop him?' "

How could it have happened?

Seventeen-year-old Ed Davies' parents wondered the same thing the day they walked into his room and found him pointing a loaded gun at his head. The Davies are committed Christians, good parents, active in their church and attentive toward their children.

It *is* happening all across our nation.

It's happening in your community.

It could happen to someone you know and love.

This book — *must* reading for every parent and responsible adult — delivers timely, crucial insight into WHY TEENS ARE KILLING THEMSELVES . . . and what we can do about it.

WHY TEENS ARE KILLING THEMSELVES

and what we can do about it

MARION DUCKWORTH

Here's Life Publishers

Published by
HERE'S LIFE PUBLISHERS, INC.
P.O. Box 1576
San Bernardino, Ca. 92402

HLP Product No. 951632

Library of Congress Cataloging-in-Publication Data
Duckworth, Marion.
      Why teens are killing themselves.
      Bibliography: p.
      1. Youth — United States — Suicidal behavior.   2. Adolescent
psychology.   3. Suicide — United States — Prevention.   4. Suicide —
Religious aspects — Christianity.
HV6546.D82   1987   362.2   86-22765
ISBN 0-89840-169-0 (pbk.)

FOR MORE INFORMATION, WRITE:

L.I.F.E. — P.O. Box A399, Sydney South 2000, Australia
Campus Crusade for Christ of Canada — Box 300, Vancouver, B.C., V6C 2X3, Canada
Campus Crusade for Christ — Pearl Assurance House, 4 Temple Row, Birmingham, B2 5HG, England
Lay Institute for Evangelism — P.O. Box 8786, Auckland 3, New Zealand
Great Commission Movement of Nigeria — P.O. Box 500, Jos, Plateau State Nigeria, West Africa
Campus Crusade for Christ International — Arrowhead Springs, San Bernardino, CA 92414, U.S.A.

To our youth

Contents

Acknowledgments

Thanks to Dr. Victor Victoroff, professional counselors Cathy Benitez, Bill Davis, Ruth McEwen, Jim Taylor, and Jane Wolf; youth ministers Morris Dirks and Rick Baylor; and Salem, Oregon, Mid-Valley Youth for Christ/Campus Life Director Rodney Berg. I am deeply grateful to the personnel of numerous suicide prevention organizations for their help. To editor Liz Duckworth for the resources she provided. To the youth who told me about the times they were suicidal. To the parents of teens who have taken their own lives, who shared their heartbreak with me, I express my appreciation.

To everyone who prayed for me while I wrote this book: *It is your book, too*.

Included in this book are accounts taken from numerous interviews I have done. I have made no attempt to comment on the individual's statements, but prefer to let the reader assess them for himself. Names and identities have been changed.

The information this book contains is given only to help individuals better understand teenage suicide. Consult a health care professional about specific behavioral problems.

About This Book

Ever since I started this project, friends have been asking, "What made you write a book about teenage suicide?" as though I'd suddenly decided to take a job at the city morgue.

I explained that when I first began reading about teen suicide in the newspaper several years ago, I wondered how the subject applied to the church of Jesus Christ. I researched more deeply and began to find answers. What I learned led me to write articles for Christian periodicals. But I could see that the subject needed a broader and deeper treatment than could be given in short pieces.

So, I tell my friends, I began to write a book.

Questions scratched at my mind as I worked. Don't people feel as though they have to deal with enough unpleasantness in life? Why should they take on any more? Is it realistic to expect the church to deal with another tough issue?

After months at work, I answered my own questions. Teen suicide is not just another problem that we can order to "Wait in line until it's your turn."

It's not just one more sign that we are in the last days. It's the result of many of the problems that are tearing our society apart. A deadly result. One Christians dare ignore no longer. An unpleasant subject? Sure. But Christians are called to wade knee-deep in unpleasantness. Jesus Christ did.

I've invited you to a funeral — to hundreds of funerals of adolescents in satin-lined coffins covered with sprays of roses. My purpose is not to panic you into a neurotic fear over the future of your kids, but to enlighten you. And then to move you to resolve to act in whatever ways the Holy Spirit shows you. May He guide you as you read.

Marion Duckworth

1

TEEN SUICIDE: EVERYBODY'S PROBLEM

How could it have happened?

Yesterday, they were walking beside us, holding our hands and begging for a penny for the gum machine. Today, they're threatening to kill themselves.

Fifteen-year-old Tammy sat across from me in our small Bible study group. Her face was white and her voice trembled as she spoke. "I found out when I got to school yesterday. Rick killed himself. He shot himself. I couldn't believe it. Just like that. And no one seems to now why."

She kept looking at her hands folded on her lap. "I saw him just the day before in school. I keep asking myself: 'Could I have said something — done something to stop him?' "

Seventeen-year-old Ed Davies' parents wondered the same thing the day they walked into his room and found him pointing a loaded gun at his head. The Davies are committed Christians, good parents, active in their church and attentive toward their children.

THE COLD FACTS

It *is* happening all across our nation. Suicide has leveled off at the third cause of death among young people. In the U.S., more than 5,000 youth between the ages of fifteen and twenty-four kill themselves annually. That's an average of one every 104 minutes. Besides that, mental health experts estimate that between 500,000 and two million young people attempt suicide every year — as many as 5,500 per day. Among males, the suicide rate increased 50 percent between 1970 and 1980, according to the Samaritans, one of the largest suicide prevention organizations.[1]

Frightening as the statistics are, they still don't portray the seriousness of the problem. Experts agree that the actual number of youth suicides is considerably higher. That's because parents often hide the fact that their child either made a suicide attempt or did kill himself. And unless there is clear evidence of the fact, officials do not list a death as a suicide. A teen who floors it on the freeway and smashes into a concrete wall may have done so deliberately. But unless he leaves a note, the motive can't be proven. And when a teen suicide victim does leave a note, the words are often apologetic: "I'm sorry I let you down."

WHO ARE THEY?

Some do mourn ghetto-raised drug addicts who jump from tenement rooftops and land, broken, among the sidewalk rubble; others associate teen suicide with the more extreme elements such as green-haired punk rockers. But most who take their lives are middle and upper middle-class kids like Ed. They have rooms of their own with posters of rock stars eyeing one another from their walls in suburban neighborhoods or suburban apartment complexes. They go to school and drive cars and stop for a burger and fries after the basketball game. Their hair is "styled," not "cut," and the jeans they wear have the correct labels.

They may hang an "everything's fine" sign on their faces, but inside, where they think and feel, they're heavy with a deep, pervasive sense of futility, like sixteen-year-old Sally who attempted suicide just before Christmas.

They kill themselves most often between three P.M.

and midnight in their own homes by using guns and by hanging themselves. They do it, not because they want to die, but because they want the pain of living to go away. They think they have no other choice. Their suicide attempts are rightly called "cries of help." *Don't you see how desperate I am?* According to Pamela Cantor, psychologist and president of the American Association of Suicidology, "They are looking down a long, dark tunnel and all they see is darkness."[2]

MORE THAN STATISTICS

Still, we find it hard to believe that suicide-prone teens could be among the ones we see strolling in shopping centers near home or in the bleachers watching a basketball game. "Not these," we think. "These are normal, happy youngsters."

Even though I'd researched the subject, I was holding on to that idea myself. Then, one of my sons brought home a copy of the paper from the high school he'd attended.

The account described the suicide death of a sophomore student. He was in good academic standing and was involved in school activities. Someone who knew him well described him as an intellectual with a sense of humor.

But the newspaper account went on to say that little things — like the quality of his handwriting — bothered him.

The teenager had been in a state of depression and under a doctor's care. At the time of his death, doctors were adjusting his medication.

As I read the story, I suddenly gasped. The boy's girlfriend was related to a friend of mine.

Besides that, the youth had gone to the same high school my own three sons had attended. They walked the same corridors, ate lunch in the same cafeteria. He played in band concerts the way one of my own sons had. They could even have sat in the same section because they played the same type of instrument.

Now, teen suicide was more than facts and figures I'd uncovered in my research. The kids who pull the trigger or careen their cars over an embankment because they are so desperate that death seems the only option, had taken on flesh and bones and breath. Teen suicide was no longer a 20th-century horror out there like world hunger. It had invaded my cloister.

I couldn't have changed what happened to that teenager. I didn't know him personally. But hearing of his death made me realize that people in my particular world *are* vulnerable.

They are in yours, too. You may be a parent or you may not. But even if you don't have children in the vulnerable years, there are youth in your world who could become statistics.

Who are they?

Make a list of teens you know who fall into the following categories:

Immediate family.

Extended family (nieces and nephews, cousins).

Friends.

Neighbors.

Church associates.

Would you know if one of them were among the plethora who are thinking about suicide? Are you one who denies that Christian kids, church-going kids, ones from good homes, can be suicidal? What are the reasons one of them could be contemplating taking his own life without you knowing? Are the reasons valid?

A DISEASE OF THE HUMAN SPIRIT

Psychologist Nancy Kehoe, who found in her research that colleagues seldom queried patients about religion, asks a pertinent question. "Why, in the face of suicide, which is a person's ultimate statement about life and death, do we separate mental health and belief?"[3]

At its roots, teen suicide is a spiritual disease. That's why non-Christian experts do not have the capability to deal with teen suicide as a disease of the human spirit, and the church has done little to address the issue.

That's *us*. Christians, if anyone, ought to be the bearers of hope. We can do something to reverse the trend that's causing youth to opt for death because they're caught in a downward descent with nothing to hold on to — no viable faith, no God who is real, no anticipation of good. So they scream for help the only way they see open to them.

We who have Christ as our hope must take the initiative and provide the help they need. For some it's too late. Fourteen-year-old Melissa Putney was one of them.

Melissa was baptized at Community Baptist Church, a one-room church on a hillside a few miles away in Joppa, Maryland. The Rev. Alpheus Jones remembers "a very lovely person. She'd always come to church, and when my wife wasn't in the choir they'd sit together."

Melissa was pregnant and she'd dropped out of church. When she was nearly due to deliver, she tidied her room and emptied her school locker and wrote a note to her mother: "You always ask me if there's anything wrong. I said, 'No, I'm OK.'

"Mom, I wasn't telling the truth. I was never OK. I was very depressed.

"I ran away from all of my problems. I am taking the easy way out."

Fourteen-year old Melissa kneeled between the rails and clasped her hands in prayer as Amtrack 141 roared toward her. The train engineer, with a young daughter of his own, saw Melissa cross herself as he applied the brakes. It was, of course, too late.

When her pastor heard the news, he said, "This is a need I'm sorry hadn't been brought to me at all. If I had known something about it earlier . . ."[4]

2

WHY NOW?

I remember vividly my feelings of shock the moment I heard the news: "Patricia tried to kill herself. She slit her wrists."

Pat was a friend of mine during my teenage years. And while I was feeling successful because I'd been hired as a radio operator at a good salary, Pat was at home shut up inside herself with a private misery.

I knew she had trouble handling her feelings and would sometimes lash out in anger. But to attempt suicide?

I was shocked not only that she'd do something so drastic, but also because when this happened four decades ago, suicide among youth was such a rarity.

Why? What has changed in our world since then? What are the external forces that are driving our children to deadly desperation?

Could the opinion of one teen be correct — that life today is tougher for kids than adults realize, that their problems are serious ones and may even top those which adults face?

We probably doubt it. Mortgage payments and job cutbacks versus chemistry exams and Friday's game against

South High? They have security — a roof over their heads, three square meals a day and a well-stocked refrigerator to raid. We're the ones who have to worry about providing it.

"You think you have it tough now," we tell them. "Just wait."

Still, none of us really knows what it's like to be a teen today. I realized that I certainly didn't several years ago when I joined a berry picking crew with my three sons during harvest here in the Northwest.

I was the only adult in the field, a silent observer in the youthful microcosm. The young people talked openly despite my presence, probably because I was dressed in berry-stained jeans the way they were and was intent only on filling my crate. Over the sound of rock music on their portable radios, I listened to accounts of last night's party and the arguments they'd had with their folks. It was as though we'd been living on separate floors of the same building. Now, for two weeks, I was looking out of their windows.

A SECULAR SOCIETY

Their world is completely secularized. Traces of God have been removed as though He were leaven and the judicial system were orthodox Jews preparing for Passover. Every day, five days a week, the average teen spends about six hours in an institution where even a moment of silence is suspect.

For God is a religious word and religion is anathema. Creationism is, too, so it's likely that the teacher's explanation of the origin of the species is Darwinian. Religion and the schools have been divorced and the Bride and all her paraphernalia have been sent packing.

In many public schools youth *are* being subtly guided to set their own moral standards, but without moral absolutes on which to base them, through "therapy education." Also called "values clarification" and "behavior modification," these courses are "an attempt, especially by counselors or health-care teachers, to help their students determine the beliefs, values and attitudes the young people hold."[1]

Add to that the fact that today's teens have teethed on the atheistic existential proposition that Dr. James Sire describes in his study of world views: "Matter exists eternally: God does not exist."[2] All this has produced a nihilistic/atheistic existential religious environment with a philosophy expressed succinctly by a youth I saw on television getting his hair mowed into a punk style: "I don't care. No one cares."

Their environment is polluted with hopelessness, but it also is exploding with violence. At prime time on TV, death is commonplace. Assault, rape and murder while they do their homework drives home the message, "Life is meaningless. Violence is in." "Dead teenager films," as one critic called movies like the *Halloween* series, do the same thing. Dismemberment and disemboweling is Saturday night fun.

HEAVY METAL

Preoccupation with death has invaded the rock scene. At least one couple feels the music their child listened to affected them in a deadly fashion. On October 26, 1984, the Jack McCollums' nineteen-year-old son, John, shot and killed himself while listening to music by rock star Ozzie Osborne. John's parents sued Osborne and the company that recorded his music. Particularly in question was his song, "Suicide Solution."

In an interview on the TV program "West 57th Street" on July 7, 1986, the McCollums' attorney, Tom Anderson, described as a born-again Christian, said he'd studied the link between heavy metal and the rise in teen suicide. "I think we have in this case opposing forces of Satan and God," he said.

The kind of music youth listen to does influence them, believes Dr. Joseph Novello, who heads up a drug program. He finds out what his patients have been playing. "Whether it's satanic, sexual or drug-oriented — it tells him [Novello] something about the child's state of mind."[3]

ROMANTICIZING SUICIDE

Experts tend to agree that certain newspaper and other reports about suicides also stimulate the depressed person to think about suicide as a way out. In fact, detailed, exploitative publicity may even contribute to a ripple effect. Within months after one youth in Clear Lake, Texas, shot himself, five others in that region followed suit. Cluster suicides have also taken place in Plano, Texas, Cheyenne, Wyoming, and upstate New York.

Teens are impressionable and news articles describing circumstances of a suicide sometimes romanticize it. Recently, a local newspaper carried an article about a couple in their seventies who "couldn't bear the thought of some day being separated or finishing out their lives in a nursing home."

The article tells how they ate a meal of foods not on their diets, drank sherry, took an overdose of medication and "lay down in each other's arms." It concludes by describing how friends and relatives joined together to remember the couple after their death by eating and drinking the foods the couple had enjoyed most.[4]

Media accounts that give instructions on methods of suicide are the most damaging of all, reports the New York State Interim Report on Youth Suicide published in December, 1985.

BREAKDOWN IN AUTHORITY

While suicide has been romanticized to teens as "the ultimate act of love," their respect for the authority figures who could provide balanced thinking has come crashing down. Edwin Newman points out that to many, the Vietnam war discredited the trustworthiness of older people because they're the ones who promoted American involvement. As a result, that "conferred a kind of blessing on youth and inexperience. . . . When age, experience and position were discredited, there was a wholesale breakdown in the enforcement of rules."[5]

Now, the rules themselves have become passé. "Thou shalt not" has become "Don't get caught." And youth aren't the only ones chanting that slogan. "Do your own thing" is often as popular with adults as with their offspring.

All this is but a shadow of the giant death that seems to be waiting in the wings — nuclear holocaust. "Let's face it," one young person told me. "The world might not even be here tomorrow." And they wonder: Are adults going to do anything about it? *Can* they do anything about it?

SEARCH FOR FAITH

Along with the breakdown in authority, the teenage years are the ones when young people begin questioning the beliefs they've been taught. Writing about youth suicide in *The*

Wall Street Journal, Steven Stack, an associate professor of sociology at Auburn University, points to the fact that there has been a steadily falling church attendance by young people, from 48 percent in 1954 to 28 percent in 1973. The same rate of decline was not true for other age groups. He points out that declining religiosity can contribute to increased suicide rates.[6]

And if they *do* go to church it is no sign that everything's fine. The mother of one teen who committed suicide told me, "He went to church with us, but he did it under protest."

If getting them to church is the ordeal of the week, we have to ask ourselves, "Why?" Are they preached at by adults who seem never to have been teens at all? Are they fed heavy-handed helpings of dogma when they're hungry to know if Jesus can help them be liked at school, get along with their parents, get a girlfriend or boyfriend? Is Christianity made to seem a religion about adults for adults? As irrelevant to them as Dad's polyester pants? If it does, they'll probably drop out as soon as they can, losing one of the few spiritual influences they have.

UNSTABLE FAMILY LIFE

The teens are years when youth are trying to separate themselves from their parents in a struggle to become adults. No longer do they want Mom and Dad to tell them what to do, but they still want and need the security of rootedness. Though they may not admit it, they want to know that they belong, that they're part of a stable family unit where people care.

But families are shattered, with one of every two couples divorced. One teenaged girl whose parents are in the process of getting a divorce said, "I feel as though I should keep my problems to myself. My folks are trying to figure out who the kids are going to live with, trying to figure out the money. I don't feel as though I can tell them how I feel about what's happening. They'll just explode and say, 'I don't have time for this.' "

Others in so-called intact homes say, "My parents are too busy working. They just don't listen to me." And many families are mobile. A teen may have been born in Arkansas, started first grade in West Virginia, and transferred schools every few years after. "It's hard if you have to move and don't know anyone in the new school," one teen told me. "I know two kids at school who moved here recently from another state. They hardly know anybody. One of them is real shy and it's hard for him to get acquainted. He gets really depressed and stays that way for a week."

SEX

Sex was rated the number one problem for a group of teens I talked with. A study of 160,000 teenagers conducted by TV producer Jane Norman and Dr. Myron Harris, a specialist in adolescent psychiatry, shows why. "Almost one out of three thirteen-to-fifteen-year-olds and six out of ten sixteen-to-eighteen-year-olds have had intercourse."[7]

"Almost everybody *is* doing it," a pretty blonde high school student told me. When Randy Alcorn, seminary faculty member, pastor and author, talked with a Christian teen about the same subject, he got the same answer:

> "Be honest with me," I said to a high school junior. "Is there *really* that much pressure to go to bed with guys?"
> "Let's put it this way," she said. "Yesterday the girl whose locker is next to mine lost her temper at another girl in our class. 'You . . . you . . . you . . . *virgin!*' She tried to think of the worst name she could call her, and she came up with 'virgin.' Does that answer your question?"[8]

DRUGS

Second and third in the list of teen problems, the group I talked with agreed, are drugs and alcohol. "Fifty-three percent of the thirteen-to-fifteen-year-olds and 78 percent of the sixteen-to-eighteen-year-olds say they drink whiskey, beer or wine occasionally," reports the Norman and Harris study. "Almost three quarters of the high schoolers say they have tried marijuana. 'It's not even the "in" thing anymore,' explains one fourteen-year-old. 'It's just part of everybody's life, almost.' "

BRINGING IT HOME

How much do you know about the entertainment available to teens in your area? Browse the newsstand for magazines with photos and stories of rock stars that describe their music and their personal lives. Look for magazines like *Winner*, *Hit Parade*, *Metal*, *Spin* and *Rock Scene*. Scan rock music lyric magazines. Look for sexually explicit periodicals like *Hustler* and *Penthouse*.

Sit through some steamy afternoon and evening soap operas. Read movie magazines. Be sure to note information about content: nudity, raw language, explicit sexual scenes including homosexual and lesbian encounters, sado-masochism, etc. Sit through as much as you can stand of an uncut movie advertised as "for mature audiences only" shown on a TV station in your area.

Browse in a record shop. Note record jackets and posters.

Stop at novelty racks you normally avoid that sell sexually explicit greeting cards and other items — sections in stores not off limits to minors.

In what ways is their world more X-rated than you imagined?

3

WHY TEENS?

Not only do teens face overwhelming external pressures, but they face them at a time when they must also cope with enormous internal pressures as well. Professional counselor Bill Davis says, "A child is going through one of the most stressful times in his or her life with the least amount of equipment to handle it."

Teens are adolescents (a word that denotes change) who are internally in a state of flux. If, at the same time, external circumstances are unstable, the results can sometimes be devastating.

The inner turmoil of adolescence doesn't come on suddenly, when a child blows out the candles on his fifteenth birthday and enters the high-risk age group. Those inner changes have been happening slowly during the metamorphosis known as puberty.

Former associate professor of psychology Luella Cole and children's social worker Irma Hall define it as "The relatively brief period of physiological change during which the sexual organs become mature. For girls this period is hardly more than six months in length, but for boys it may last two years

27

or even longer. Puberty supplies the basis for adolescence but is by no means synonymous with it."[1]

It's important that adults understand what puberty is all about. Although the suicide rate during those years is considerably lower than for older teens, what happens during those years greatly influences the way they handle adolescence. Are they developing self-understanding? And the ability to cope with their changing selves? Unless adults understand, they can't help youth adjust. In their ignorance, adults can make things worse.

PUBERTY'S MILESTONES

One of the first signs may be awkwardness around the opposite sex. Girls develop breasts and go shopping with Mom for their first bra. Menstruation begins, an experience so profound that most remember where they were and what they were doing when it happened. For those who have been prepared it is an exciting rite of passage. Others whose parents have been tongue-tied about sex may experience extreme anxiety.

"My mother never explained menstruation and acted like something terrible had happened to me," Cathy explains.

Nina remembers: "I did everything I could to hide the fact that I was developing because my folks acted like sex was bad. So becoming a woman made me feel guilty."

During male puberty, a boy notices marked growth of the penis and scrotum. He may experience his first nocturnal emission, as well as almost daily arousal as he wonders about the overwhelming sensations his body is discovering. Both sexes develop pubic and axillary hair. Both experience growth spurts that leave parents sighing and shaking their heads and teens wondering who in the world they are becoming.

This is the age of sexual experimentation and the formation of sexual identity. Many youth — both boys and girls — practice masturbation. From the time we sat them as babies in the bathtub they discovered their genital area with curiosity. Now, they are discovering that self-stimulation is pleasurable.

They are trying desperately to fit into this new body of theirs. *Who in the world am I now?* They may feel guilty if they are masturbating, if they have sexual fantasies, and if they've been giving in to the enormous urge to look at sexually explicit magazines on the supermarket rack (and may even have some hidden in the back of their closet). Many begin to live dual lives now — the interior one in which they're struggling to deal with their sexuality and changing body and the external one they show to adults — a fact that only adds to the already growing pressure within.

Hormones secreted into the teenage body cause volatile emotional changes. Psychologist Bruce Narramore points out: "The fundamental physical changes of teenage life do not influence only our teenagers' body size and shape, but their emotional stability and adjustment as well."[2]

EMOTIONAL CHANGES

Emotional energy builds up within and explodes at the dinner table, or in the car on the way to church. It is "a stirred-up state of the entire organism," explain Cole and Hall.[3] Adrenalin is secreted and discharged by glands into the blood stream. It may retard the digestive process. Salivary glands cease to function. The heart beats faster. Sweat glands function. Tears flow. Males experience sudden erections.

When teens get up to give an oral report, undress during P.E., compete on the athletic field, they experience a variety of uncomfortable emotional responses. If the teen is laughed at or put down, if additional stress is heaped on during already stressful times and no experienced, sensitive adult is alongside to listen and understand, the teen may feel like a bubbling cauldron inside.

That's the way Jim felt. The baby of the family, his mother was reluctant to let him develop independence. Parenting had given her a sense of worth, so she clung to the fifteen-year-old, still calling him baby names, treating him as though he were an extension of herself. Sometimes, Jim hated his mother. When that happened, he felt sick with guilt.

Both of Marge's parents were college professors. They expected her to become a professional like themselves. When her report cards didn't boast top grades, they'd sigh disappointedly. Sensing her inability to measure up, Marge became more and more depressed and unable to concentrate. She withdrew into her room and plugged into the world of raucous rock where her parents couldn't follow.

INTELLECTUAL CHANGES

Along with his physical and emotional development, a teen is learning to think, to reason and to rationalize. And he wants to think for himself.

He has a lot to think about and he's probably working hard at it, although he may not seem to be. *What am I going to be? How can I get her to notice me? Why can't I convince my parents that I can decide things for myself?*

If his basic human need for security, love, acceptance, friendship, belonging, recognition and accomplishment aren't being realized (because of problem parents, societal rejection, poverty, abuse or some other reason), he spends long hours trying to figure out what's wrong and what to do about it.

But although his reasoning powers are developing rapidly, he does not have the insight or perspective that years will bring to help him do so. He may conclude, therefore, that if his life is wrong somehow because it doesn't follow the norm (he has an alcoholic father, a neurotic mother), that *he* somehow is wrong — a person for whom the world has no place.

PERSONHOOD

At the same time, he's trying to take the pieces of himself and put them together into a whole: A physical appearance with which he is comfortable. An emotional disposition that expresses his true inner nature. A mind that can think through the issues that smack him in the face and provide satisfactory answers. A personality that is genuine.

That takes a lot of internal peering, trying on images and discarding them and then trying on new ones. Someone once said, "Don't laugh at a youth for his affectations: He is only trying on one face after another to find a face of his own."

He is asking *the* question: *"Who am I?"* His first answer, says professional counselor Bill Davis, is a negative one: *"I don't know who I am, but I'm not you."* He says it somewhere between ages twelve and fourteen. That's part of the process taking place within — the natural, internal pressure to become an independent person separate from his parents. He's uncertain and looks cautiously around to see how his struggle to be independent is being received, anxious to know whether he's still loved.

"By age fifteen to eighteen," Davis goes on, "he's ready to build a positive identity. He begins to cultivate his own interests — in athletics, academics. The individual begins to set a pattern of *'Who I am'* that usually carries into his twenties."

The self he needs most to discover is the hardest to come by. It is his spiritual identity. If he has embraced a personal God, he probably questions Him now: *Does God really know me?*

LET TEENS TELL IT

What's it like to be a teen? Listen to what they have to say about some of the subjects we've covered. Here are some actual quotes from a teenage roundtable discussion I sat in on:

Sex: "Kids don't get love at home so they substitute sex."

"Some kids use sex the way they use drugs and alcohol. It provides a different kind of high."

Disillusionment: "People lie to you. You give someone money to get a keg of beer and they tell you it costs more than it really does and use the extra to get something for themselves. People lie to you all the time."

"You have two-faced friends. You tell them something personal. It's important to you but they may think it's dumb and tell someone else and make a big joke out of it."

Rejection: "Friends reject you. You try to talk to someone and they walk away. People keep treating you like you don't belong."

"Something goes wrong in a friendship. You keep asking yourself: Is it me? What's wrong with me?"

Parents: "You'd like to talk to them but they don't listen."

"I can't talk to my folks. They'd wig out if they knew."

What would they tell their parents? "We're not faking it. We need help."

"Help me know what to do. My mom talks to me, but when we're done, I still don't know what to do."

"Put yourself in our place. How would you react?"

BRINGING IT HOME

Try it. Do put yourself in their place. Maybe you can't join a strawberry picking crew the way I did (or maybe you can).

How *can* you become a teen for a day — or an hour? Sit in a back booth at their favorite hang-out. Listen and learn. Throw a party for teens in your church or neighborhood on the next holiday and pay attention while you hand out punch and popcorn. Help with a paper drive or whatever teen activity comes along.

But none of it will do any good unless you do it empathetically. That means you'll have to "project your personality" into the personality of a teen in order to understand him better. Remember that a teen has changed internally from child to adult. He (you) are living in a sexually explicit, erotic era where boundaries have been pulled up, family life torn down and religious faith shoved to the back of the bus.

How *would* you react?

4

DEPRESSION

In the grim grip of
Deadly, debilitating depression
I hopelessly hide myself.
Life brightly beckons
Confusing me with a colorful come-on.
My spirit struggles
But I am as a stone and
Do not respond to lusty life's false front.
But for that little spark of spirit
I would be safe in my secluded cell.
No strife. No struggle.
NO RISK!
Entombed — immured — secure in
A cocoon so cunningly
Wrapped 'round and 'round
I've traded effort and energy
For ennui.

The young woman who wrote these words (an excerpt from her poem) and gave me permission to include them in this book, began to experience depression when she was in grade school. Eventually, she attempted suicide. Even now, years later, she's plagued with bouts of depression when her self-worth slides to zero and her will to live wavers precariously.

Psychiatrists Griest and Jefferson point out that "About three-quarters of the people who kill themselves are depressed at the time they do so. Feelings of helplessness or hopelessness or worthlessness or guilt about some real or imagined fault often lead to thoughts of suicide."[1]

Usually, such depression comes on slowly. Professional counselor Jane Wolf explains: "Teens come to a point where they feel things are never going to get any better. As in any depression, the past is interpreted as bad, the present is dark and so is the future." To show how desperate they are, they may make suicidal gestures or genuine attempts. For that reason, it's vital for those closely associated with teens to be able to recognize signs of serious depression.

A youth worker I talked with remembered his own serious depression not long after he emerged from his teens. "I literally felt as though I was going through hell on earth. I was a Christian but I couldn't get a handle on my faith. I wouldn't kill myself, but I asked God to take something else from me — an arm, a leg, instead — and give me back my mental health." Finally, he went to a pastor and then a psychologist and received the help he needed to get well.

Depression (from "to press down") is a state of lowered spirits that affects thoughts, feelings, and bodily functions and causes changes in behavior. Specifically, Greist and Jefferson say, "When we diagnose *depression*, we mean a disorder of sufficient length with specific symptoms and signs which substantially interferes with a person's functioning or which causes great personal distress — or both."[2]

Everyone — teenagers especially — have times when they see the world in shades of gray. "I spent the whole game on the bench — again. The other kids make fun of me." But a new sunrise, a new game ("I got to play and I made four points!") and the world is splashed with streaks of gold again.

But when they are clinically depressed, they're experiencing more than a passing low mood. One woman who experienced it describes it this way: "There's no love. There's no hope, no joy. And the only thing [you feel] is that terrible fear and an awful desire to die."[3]

When asked in a TV interview why she attempted suicide, a high school girl described a not uncommon story. Her parents were going through divorce and relationships at home were bad. She got in with the wrong crowd and started using drugs. "I was two different people at home and at school." Her attitudes communicated her feelings that "I don't care." Finally, she attempted suicide.

A counselor who spoke afterward said, " 'I don't care' may be a young person's way of being angry. *You need me to care, so I'll show you.'* The suicide attempt can be a way of getting even."

The most common element in suicide is depression, he said, and described that state similar to looking out a window with a shade over it. You can see outside but things don't seem really clear to you.

FACTS ABOUT TEENAGE DEPRESSION

This kind of depression can be reactive — triggered by a specific trauma in the life of the individual. Or, serious depression can come from unknown causes within and may even be recurring, the way it has been for the young woman who wrote the poem that began this chapter.

Depressed youth are often angry. They may feel guilty, too. As one counselor put it, anger turned inward, against the self, causes depressive feelings.

One sixteen-year-old boy admits that's what happened to him when he was fifteen. "I was angry — angry at my parents, my friends, myself, and the whole world . . . I was angry at my real parents for bringing me into the world . . . I was angry at my adoptive parents for bringing me into their home."

He started taking drugs to escape. Then, one Saturday night around midnight, he took forty-five pills. "I then waited to die."

Fortunately, he did reach for the phone and called for help. Six months' treatment in a Christian mental hospital helped him deal with his feelings. Now, he says, "No matter what, suicide is not the answer."[4]

Teens do not always act the way adults do when they're depressed — sitting lethargically, with misery etched on their faces. Instead, they may mask their feelings so they don't seem depressed at all. They may display a variety of behavior problems. They may talk back, defy rules, abuse drugs and alcohol, or be sexually promiscuous.

A clinically depressed youth may become suicidal. Most of us think about death sometime. We may even think in passing that those who are plaguing us with problems might see how unfair they've been if they were standing over our coffin. I remember writing in my own diary when I was a teenager and angry at my mother, "She'd be sorry if I was dead." But for a seriously depressed youth, the thought of suicide is ongoing and if help is not forthcoming, he may become convinced it's the only way out. The following are common reasons for depression.

A SIGNIFICANT LOSS

Loss of self worth. "This factor keeps coming up over and over. They don't measure up — don't have what it takes," Jane Wolf says.

For one girl I know, it was because she was much taller than the others in her class. Because she was bigger, adults expected more out of her than she was capable of producing. They stopped giving her the physical affection she craved — because "You're a big girl now." As a result, she felt different, unacceptable.

For another, it was a physical handicap that was the result of an accident when she was a child. The sense of rejection, because her family felt they couldn't care for her anymore, produced a smoldering anger.

For others I know, the problem was a learning disability. Still stumbling through textbooks when others were reading easily. Or having an unusually high I.Q. and being singled out as a super-brain.

A loss in family life. Divorce. Loss of closeness due to chaos in a family at a time when youth need a stable home base. Instability because of lack of roots. Rejection or abuse by a parent.

When his father left and his mother became preoccupied with her own problems, Cliff felt alone and terribly afraid. When he made a suicide attempt, his mother realized how hard hit he was and sought out professional help.

Loss of security. While a teen *wants* to become an independent adult, he still wants to do it at a pace he can handle. If parents take hands off, making him feel he's being abandoned and must work things out for himself, if all the old securities of knowing what the limits are suddenly vanish, the result can be frightening for a teen.

As the youth steps toward adulthood, he still wants to maintain bonding with his parents. If he senses that relationship diminishing significantly now that he's an adolescent, he may mourn.

Loss of reputation. Embarrassment before peers because a romantic interest drops him when self-esteem is low already and when other relationships are hanging by a thread can be a significant factor.

In *The Urge to Die,* Peter Giovacchini points out that the fact that a teenager loses a school election for president of his class doesn't seem like a tragedy to an adult. To a youth with a poor sense of personal worth, however, mass rejection is traumatic.

Loss of other love objects. Tracy was an outstanding, talented student in high school when she became seriously depressed. Although a number of factors contributed — a feeling of loneliness, loss of a best friend who moved away, her mother's accident — it was the loss of her cat Emmy that was the last straw.

"At least *she* seemed to listen," Tracy recalled. Tracy stopped attending school, and her sleep patterns changed radically. She lost interest in things that were important to her before and started giving clues that she was thinking of suicide.[5]

HABITUAL NEGATIVE THINKING

Negative thinking can be a family characteristic. The youth adopts his family's pessimism toward life and interprets his own experiences that way.

A youth's emotional state may be influenced by an adult who is also depressed.

PHYSICAL-GENETIC CAUSES

Sleep, diet, etc. Teens live on the run. Professional counselor Jane Wolf sends a depressed teen for a medical checkup. She finds out what they're eating. Are they getting enough rest? They may be working hard for grades, involved in extra-curricular activities, holding down a part-time job and trying to maintain relationships at home, and are worn out.

Adults should be aware that there can be other physiological causes. Dr. Gary R. Collins mentions "the effects of drugs, low blood sugar and other chemical malfunctioning, brain tumors, or glandular disorders. Then there is research which has stressed the importance of the hypothalamus in producing depression. . . .

"Although it is not conclusive," Collins says, "there is some evidence to show that severe depression runs in families." [6]

Premenstrual tension. PMS does cause depressive feelings, we know now. One girl who wrote her first suicide note at eighteen said, "Usually around the time of my period . . . I would sit and cry for no apparent reason." [7]

DRUGS AND ALCOHOL

Not all who use drugs and alcohol do so because they are depressed, but when a teen does resort to use of these because he *is* depressed, he finds himself falling farther into the tunnel.

MENTAL ILLNESS

In rare cases, serious depression may be the result of mental illness like manic-depression. But psychotic disturbances are an infrequent cause.

UNREALISTIC EXPECTATIONS

More often, a contributing factor is pressure to succeed. One girl who was singled out publicly as an exceptional student supposed that meant she must maintain straight A's and win in everything she did. In other cases, parents' attitudes cause problems. "My father was never satisfied with what I did," a woman I know recalled. "He never complimented me. I felt worse and worse because I wanted desperately to win his approval, but I never could."

LEARNED HELPLESSNESS

When a youth thinks he's tried everything he knows and nothing works, he's bound to feel as though he's sinking in quicksand. Collins sees depression as a common response. "When we learn that our actions are futile no matter how hard we try, that there is nothing we can do to relieve suffering, reach a goal or bring change, then depression is a common response."[8]

Counselors generally agree that if a teenager shows signs of serious depression for two weeks, he or she should be taken to a health care professional for evaluation. (Youth depression and its relationship to suicidal behavior is discussed in chapter 15: "When an Emergency Strikes.")

Read the following true account and see what causes for depression you can find.

Don was a bright, ambitious boy from a close family that spent most of its free time together. As a result, he rarely socialized with others his age. He did attend church and went to some of the young people's special events. But even then, he kept to himself.

When Don was about seventeen and he became more and more reclusive, spending hours alone in his room, his parents knew he had a problem and took him to a counselor. During the therapy he graduated from high school and went to work, but kept living at home. When he was advised by someone involved in his therapy that he should move out to begin his own life, he did so.

A few days after the move, though, Don went back home where he'd grown up, probably the place he felt most safe. Locating a rifle he knew was in the house, he went to his old room, empty now except for memories, and closed the door. When his family came home, they found their son dead.

What new things have you learned about teenage depression in this chapter? Read Psalm 88:1-9 as though it were written by a depressed adolescent, and capture his feelings.

It's usually not a single cause that pushes youth to depression and suicidal tendencies. And not every young person responds the same way to the same set of circumstances. Depressed adolescents may not *mean* to kill themselves, only show how badly they hurt by inflicting an ugly, gaping wound like the one they feel inside.

They may do so to manipulate their parents, to make another person feel sorry for real or imagined injustices, to avoid consequences of some action. They may think they want to die to be with someone who's already dead. They may be trying to get what they want, like the young man I know who called the girl who'd stopped seeing him and said he had a gun and would kill himself unless she took him back. When she faltered, he did pull the trigger, wounding himself.

Some of the most chilling reports of suicides are by teens who were involved in Satanism and occult-type games. Psychologist Emery Nester, writing about depression and suicide, says, "Let's consider the matter of Satan's direct involvement in suicide. Surely every attack of depression is not demonic. We have talked about biochemical irregularities, environmental factors and internal personal dynamics as sufficient cause for a person to be depressed. Even suicide can be free from Satan's direct influence.

"On the other hand, special demonic activity can bring about the possibility of losses, hindered or hampered relationships, or other situations which could cause depression. Satan's involvement as the 'god of this age' can also create pressures at a time of deep depression which may encourage one to end his life." [9]

To reverse the awful trend of teenage suicide, we'll have to do more than tut and cluck and shake our heads over a generation that's gone to the dogs. Do more than ask, "What's the matter — why don't they appreciate everything they've got?" Or pronounce piously that if they'd only accept Jesus as their Savior these things wouldn't happen.

Many of the youth who have attempted to kill themselves *are* Christians. And of the three major religious groups, Protestants have the highest rate of teen suicide.

Even Christian kids can become as bone dry of hope as all the rest.

BRINGING IT HOME

Have you ever been depressed? What were the reasons? How do you feel about people who are depressed — are you understanding or impatient? What determines your response to them? Do you believe "spiritual" people don't get depressed?

What kind of response do you appreciate most when you are feeling down? Have you had preconceptions about teenage depression you need to reexamine? What things made you feel miserable when you were a teenager? Ask teens you know what kinds of things get them down.

5

CHRISTIANS: LEADERS OF THE PACK

Bone dry of hope. That's the way the apostles felt when Jesus lay in His rock tomb. That's the way Mary Magdalene, Joanna, Mary the mother of James and the others found the apostles when they came running with the news, "Jesus has risen."

Only Peter and John ran to the tomb to examine the strips of cloth in which Jesus' body had been wrapped. Even then the apostles didn't smack their foreheads and exclaim, *Of course. How could we have been so stupid?* John notes: "They still did not understand from Scripture that Jesus had to rise from the dead" (John 20:9).

NEEDED: PEOPLE WITH HOPE

To the depressed, hope never comes easily. It's hard to believe life can be cheers and applause again when your heart is leaden. That's especially true of youth who are not far enough down the road to look back at the ruts *and* the sun-splashed rises of life.

Like Peter and the others, they need someone already convinced — someone who knows — that *Jesus is alive* — *His promises are true*. They need adults who see with spiritual eyes, who hear with spiritual ears, who know that God and not nuclear weapons is in control.

"Imagine what it must be like for them," one mother challenged me. "Imagine discussions of a nuclear war in a school setting where God and His plan are never mentioned. Then, there are all the other subjects like crime, terrorism, world hunger. They come away feeling miserable about life."

The answer? Easy, we think. Give them the gospel like a good dose of tonic to take away the winter blahs. As though it were a magic remedy that, once ingested, neutralizes disillusionment and despair.

But it's not that simple. And teens are wary. Is the Christian message ancient history or current events? Does it work? Are the ones who speak the message whole themselves? Able to cope? Do they sing "Jesus is the joy of living," but live one-dimensional lives as though matter is the only reality? Do they talk God and church youth group but spit embitterment because of their head-on collisions with the world? Have they taught a "toe the mark" religion and presented God as a Divine Policeman who is carefully writing down every infringement?

The breathing dead, as Hal Lindsey refers to those without hope, will not be fooled by corpses mouthing religious messages. They will only settle for Hope Himself. And, like Thomas, they must see Him to believe.

Not the man Christ, walking through locked doors, but the Spirit of Christ indwelling their parents and brothers and sisters, extended family, teachers, church leaders and friends. Hope-filled because they are Spirit-filled. Not handing out a message as though it were medicine to cure their ills, but demonstrating "Christ in you, the hope of glory" (Colossians 1:27).

He is the one who inbreathes hope. He uses no heavenly voodoo to do the job, but His Spirit through "the church, which is his body, the fullness of him" (Ephesians 1:22, 23).

We are the ones who are called to come alongside, much the way my husband Jack did the night he received the phone call that the infant son of friends had stopped breathing. Jack was a volunteer fireman in the small community where we live, and he was trained in CPR. Jack rushed over, placed his mouth over the baby's tiny one, and began exhaling his own inner life into the still child. All during the thirty-five-mile trip to the hospital, Jack stood by, giving resuscitation when it was needed.

The baby began to breathe. Little shallow gasps at first. Then more regularly. Color returned to tiny cheeks. "Saving a life," Jack remembers, "there's no experience in the world like it."

The hope we're called to inbreathe is the genuine kind, not its slicked-up, 20th-century counterpart, defined as "a feeling that what is wanted will happen,"[1] which is no hope at all. The biblical version of hope is the ability to anticipate every day on earth with confidence. Because that's what real hope is: an attitude of expectancy, of faith. The ability to live in peace and wait patiently because we know the sons of God will be revealed (Romans 8:19).

THE SOURCE OF HOPE

But the definition youth ache to hear most, perhaps, is one Hal Lindsey describes: *Chasah*. "Its root meaning is 'to seek shelter, refuge or protection in something or someone.' It is used frequently to portray little animals taking refuge in the cleft of a rock. . . . Figuratively it came to be used of man's taking refuge in God from the spiritual, emotional and physical dangers of life."[2]

Hope in the Bible is not only an action or attitude of the soul or spirit. It is a noun, too — the divine noun, God Himself. "Christ Jesus our hope" (1 Timothy 1:1).

He is the ground on which our anticipation is based and the reason we can live expectantly. The resurrected Christ who demonstrated His divinity with every healing touch, who is lord of our circumstances now — He Himself is our Hope.

Peter, who knew what despair felt like, began his first letter talking about hope. "Praise be to the God and father of our Lord Jesus Christ! In his great mercy he has given us new birth into a living hope through the resurrection of Jesus Christ from the dead" (1 Peter 1:3).

So Christian optimism — based on the fact that Christ is risen — was born. Death, and all that it implies, has been conquered. The hope Peter describes is "an energizing principle,

a spontaneous, overflowing, buoyant thing. It is . . . a spirit
of optimism, a looking ever upon the bright side of things, a
looking forward to only that which is good, an expectancy of
continued blessing and joy." [3]

Not that Christian optimism comes easily. When Peter
wrote, Christians were being persecuted. "Suffering" is the key
word in his letter. Early believers were losing their homes and
becoming refugees. Still, he pressed for steady, quiet confidence
in God.

This true counterpart of its modern day imitation,
positive thinking, comes only through the new birth. "Believe
in God: believe also in Me." Spiritual life is then imparted by
the Spirit of God to man's own spirit, enabling him to know
what was only theology before.

God is real.
God is good.
God is a Person.
God cares.
God is Lord.
God will help.

This is the message of hope our youth need to see
modeled by their mentors.

"The problem is," one concerned father told me, "that
kids have been fed a line that they must be self-sufficient.
That's the philosophy of the society we live in."

Youth need to know that the world is wrong. Man
wasn't created to be self-sufficient. He was created to live in
relationship with God.

But youth need to understand what eternal life really
is. (And perhaps we do as well.) Not the cliche definition — "to
live in heaven with Jesus." The one Christ Himself gave:

"Now this is eternal life: that they may know you, the
only true God, and Jesus Christ, whom you have sent" (John
17:3).

Eternal life is friendship with God *now.* Help and hope
now. Help in understanding one's sexuality, gaining acceptance,
finding a place to belong, coping with emotional pain, finding
direction for life.

The trouble is, we may be as teenaged as our teens — as
easily influenced, as unsteady. They get their philosophy from
rock videos; we get ours from advice columns. We're not sure

ourselves what to believe, or we feel dichotomized by the church and the world about what is success and fulfillment and freedom.

WE MUST MODEL HOPE

To model hope, we must have hope ourselves. Not that we don't flounder when life smacks us in the face and we lose a job or a loved one. "If I'm expected to say 'life is swell,' forget it," an adult friend said to me. "I'm a realist. That means I face facts."

True enough. Life is *not* always swell. As I write this, people I know are suffering. The husband of one friend had his leg amputated. Another friend lost her husband, who was only thirty-five years old. Others have been abandoned by their mates, face financial disaster or loss of reputation. A child has died from a brain tumor. The husband of a writing friend has Alzheimer's disease at forty-five.

In our nation, AIDS is increasing and so is drug addiction. Pollution is turning some of our Northwest rivers gray-green and foamy. Americans are afraid to travel overseas because of international terrorism. A Russian nuclear accident sent radiation into Oregon where I live and has triggered talk of future nuclear disaster.

That's reality. So how can we be optimists?

Not by denying the reality of the kingdom of darkness. Satan and his legion do exist and so do all of the painful results of man's fall into sin.

But there's a second reality. It is the kingdom of light established by Christ who defeated death and who is its Lord. This kingdom is invisible and must be seen with one's spiritual senses.

Christ, who is Lord of the second reality, has outwitted and overpowered the ruler of the first. "The reason the Son of God appeared was to destroy the devil's work" (1 John 3:8). Those whose citizenship is in the second reality, the kingdom of light, are no longer under the dominion of the demons of the first. These live by faith that the Lord God Almighty will take the works of Satan and use them to beautify the kingdom of light because they ask Him to do so.

But that doesn't give us easy answers to the questions about pain that make youth stare, frowning at God. "How could He have let a guy in my school get shot by that crazy gunman and be permanently disabled?" "How come kids returning home in a church bus with their youth group got crushed to death in a highway accident?"

We do not have all the answers to their hard questions, or to our own, either. But "hope that is seen is no hope at all" (Romans 8:24). We wait confidently for what we do not now have, and that includes the answers to our collective "why's?"

Still, we are confident. Because, in our spirits, *we know Him* — experientially, as the one who answers our prayers, who gives strength when our own is gone.

Our youth must know Him that way, too — as the God of hope who fills them with all joy and peace as they trust in Him, so that they may overflow with hope by the power of the Holy Spirit (Romans 15:13).

WHEN WE'RE DOWN

Ginger's mother had been depressed ever since her husband walked out two years before. She refused professional help and just plodded heavily through each day. Evenings were worse. Her energy was dissipated and she sat in silence staring at the TV.

Ginger had been shattered herself when her father left. Being around her mom only made her feel worse. She wanted her mother's help, ached for the sense of security a warm relationship with her mother could provide. But her mother seemed oblivious to the girl's need.

There are times in every adult's life when he or she isn't exactly a wellspring of hope. Life is going badly. The future seems blurred, and we have hardly enough hope to keep ourselves afloat and pitifully little to give to the youth in our lives.

Don't we have a right to our down times?

Of course. But we don't have a right to muddle in our own misery until we cast a shadow wherever we walk. If we are suffering from depression ourselves, we have a responsibility to get help and be honest with the youth who sense the way we feel. And as soon as we are able, to nourish our spirits with hope again through Scriptures like the ones that follow and to teach the principles to our youth for their own down times.

***

"Praise be to the God and Father of our Lord Jesus Christ! In his great mercy he has given us new birth into a living hope through the resurrection of Jesus Christ from the dead" (1 Peter 1:3).

Peter burst with hallelujahs. Not because life was great — it wasn't. Christ's prediction of persecution was coming true fast. Praise came from Peter's spirit where he had been reborn, because he knew he was tied not to this world, but to God who had given him eternal life.

***

"For the grace of God that brings salvation has appeared to all men. It teaches us to say 'No' to ungodliness and worldly passions, and to live self-controlled, upright and godly lives in this present age, while we wait for the blessed hope — the glorious appearing of our great God and Savior, Jesus Christ" (Titus 2:11-13).

How to survive in a world ruled by the Evil One? Count on the Spirit of God and wisdom from the Word of God. Cultivate a pure life and live expecting the visible manifestation of the source of hope — Jesus Christ.

***

"May our Lord Jesus Christ himself and God our Father, who loved us and by his grace gave us eternal encouragement and good hope, encourage your hearts and strengthen you in every good deed and word" (2 Thessalonians 2:16, 17).

God gave us hope when He gave us His Son. He is the eternal encourager. Go to Him and He will fill your spirit with Himself.

***

"But now he has reconciled you by Christ's physical body through death to present you holy in his sight, without blemish and free from accusation — if you continue in your faith, established and firm, not moved from the hope held out in the Gospel" (Colossians 1:22,23).

No matter what happens, we are asked to choose to keep believing that: (1) God is a loving, caring Father; (2) Christ is our substitute; (3) He will present us to the Father as pure as though we were fresh-made in Eden; (4) Christ is preparing to welcome us into the indestructible kingdom.

***

"To them God has chosen to make known among the Gentiles the glorious riches of this mystery, which is Christ in you, the hope of glory" (Colossians 1:27).

Rejoice in God's inclusiveness. In the fact that you can be intimate with Him *now.* His presence is like a photo over the fireplace with a note at the bottom: "I love you."

***

"For everything that was written in the past was written to teach us, so that through endurance and the encouragement of the Scriptures we might have hope" (Romans 15:4).

How is hope produced? By choosing to keep going the way Jesus did in Gethsemane because you're determined to finish the race. And by accepting God's written promises as true and counting on them.

***

"A faith and knowledge resting on the hope of eternal life, which God, who does not lie, promised before the beginning of time" (Titus 1:2).

This kind of hope won't be shattered. That's because it is based on the promises of one who simply does not lie. And His offer of union with Him is no afterthought, thrown casually to mankind as part of some eternal bonus plan. It was planned by Him even before He invented days and hours and minutes and seconds.

***

"The former regulation is set aside because it was weak and useless (for the law made nothing perfect), and a better hope is introduced, by which we draw near to God" (Hebrews 7:18, 19).

Some days, we feel completely unacceptable. Those are the times grace astounds us most. *I can humble myself before God. And He'll be there, open-armed, like the prodigal's father.* Not because we kept all the rules or offered the right sacrifice. Only because we are in Christ.

***

"Through him you believe in God, who raised him from the dead and glorified him, and so your faith and hope are in God" (1 Peter 1:21).

No matter how many tricks we invent to cheer ourselves up — to lift our spirits — the only solid conviction that wrong will be righted is based on His Word.

***

"Therefore, prepare your minds for action; be self-controlled; set your hope fully on the grace to be given you when Jesus Christ is revealed" (1 Peter 1:13).

The ability to live as a Christian optimist begins in your mind. How are you thinking? On what are you focusing? Do your thoughts wander like vagrants? Peter urges us, by the power of the Holy Spirit, to grab our mind by the nape of the neck and plunk it where it belongs. When it wanders, like a vagrant does, bring it back. And set your thoughts on God's grace. Expect Him to perform acts of kindness and look for "more of God's kindness to you when Jesus Christ returns."

***

"May the God of hope fill you with all joy and peace as you trust in him, so that you may overflow with hope by the power of the Holy Spirit" (Romans 15:13).

Make this a personal prayer. Put it in the first person. Breathe it to God, sigh it to Him, weep it when human love swings around and slaps you in the face. For always, God urges you back home again into His presence so that you can overflow with hope by the power of the Spirit of God and warm the lives of the despairing youth who people your world.

BRINGING IT HOME

Meditate during your daily quiet time on the preceding Scriptures. Put them in your own words. Ask yourself: *What do they say and what do they say to me?* Write ones that mean the most to you on cards and memorize them by displaying them in places where you'll see them often. Isolate the key phrase in each that helps you have hope. Use them as foundations for your prayers so you can learn to live in hope and to reflect an attitude of hope to the youth in your world.

6

A CHANGE OF ATTITUDE

When I heard that the high school department in my church needed teachers, I debated whether to volunteer. One of my own sons was a high school student then, so the ways of youth were fresh in my mind. I should know how to talk teenage, to gear the gospel for their ears with illustrations of Darth Vader and The Force. Besides, hadn't I had plenty of experience? Hadn't I taught teens frequently during the eleven years my husband had been a minister?

That first Sunday, feeling like a frightened freshman, I walked into the large room where dozens of young people and their teachers met to socialize before class. They stood around in knots of teens and adults, throwing their heads back with laughter, slapping one another good naturedly on the shoulder.

I hung back by the door, looking for a familiar face. Except for a couple of teachers (my own son wasn't there that day), they were people I knew only by sight. *You should walk up to a group, smile dazzlingly, say hi, introduce yourself and talk baseball games and the weekend snow trip.* Instead, I slipped as quietly as I could into a seat in the back row and tried to look calm and at ease.

The Sunday social time wasn't any easier for me even after I learned the names and faces of the twenty or so teens in my class. But the forty-five minutes I stood before the group teaching Hebrews, I loved. Up front, where I was in charge, I was comfortable. No one-on-one confrontations in which I might falter and act like a dumb adult. Capturing their attention, drawing them into the discussion, was what I was good at.

They seemed to like the way I taught. One student even told me so. *If only we could leave it at that,* I kept thinking every Saturday night as I got my material together. *Just go in the classroom, teach the lesson and leave.* But I was supposed to get to know them, too, and on that score I was failing badly.

The reason mingling was so hard for me was because of my own painful teenage years. Every Sunday at 9:45 A.M., I felt as though I were walking through the door of my own high school, facing kids who stood in knots whispering to one another. They never stopped to motion me toward them. They walked to class together, calling to one another, "See you." I'd walk alone or with another like myself who lived on the fringes.

That had been nearly thirty years ago, but my subconscious mind hadn't grown up: *Teens rejected you then; they'll reject you now.* It wasn't until somewhere near the end of my tenure as a teacher in the high school department that my attitude began to change slightly.

That happened on a Sunday evening. The high schoolers were having a social that I said I'd attend. One of the boys in my class had room in his car and motioned for me to climb in beside him. On the way, we talked about Sunday school and he side-glanced at me. "You're OK . . . I can talk to you," he blurted out.

I felt as though I'd just been handed the Sunday school award of the year.

Because one teen accepted me instead of rejecting me the way others had done in 1943, I felt more at ease with the whole group. By the end of my teaching year, I had gained enough confidence in their acceptance of me to walk up to a knot of kids during the Sunday social hour with a reasonable degree of confidence.

Preconceptions based on early experiences that make us conclude, "Teens don't like me," aren't the only problem. A variety of other ideas about teens are loose in adult society as well.

Good guys and bad guys. This kind of thinking puts kids in tight compartments. Good guys sit sedately in the sanctuary with Bibles on their lap. They have after-school jobs and mow the lawn on Saturday.

Bad guys walk with swaggers and carry ghetto blasters.

Airheads. This viewpoint implies that most kids don't have a serious thought in their head. This group sees teenage as one big joke about voracious appetites and video games and manipulating parents for the keys to the car.

A different breed. "They have a language, clothes and interests all their own. You have to be a parent or a teacher to figure them out. Anyway, they *want* to be left alone. As far as they're concerned, adults are only a nuisance."

The "Father Knows Best" fantasy. These are the people who still see teens as they were in the "Leave It to Beaver" era. Boys with neatly trimmed hair, girls with pony tails, both sexes dressed in clothes like the ones in the catalog. Teens around the table at dinner every night at six passing bowls of mashed potatoes and platters of roast beef and talking with parents who have plenty of time to listen. These teens' biggest dilemmas are whether to take the ugly family friend to the prom or whether to tell Mom "I'm sorry. I borrowed your pink sweater without asking and ruined it."

Extended childhood. They play with bigger toys and decide whether to date Charlie or Greg instead of whether to play cops and robbers or house. They eat more and cost more but they're still just big kids who over-dramatize what's going on.

Not my responsibility. This is one of the most dangerous. "I raised my kids/don't have any kids. Let their parents, teachers and pastor worry about them. I've got enough problems trying to run my own life. I take care of my own and everyone else should do the same thing."

This one is communicated more by deed than word. Not a W.C. Fields brush-off, "Go away, kid, you bother me." Instead, it's indicated by shrugs when the youth department asks for volunteers.

How do you view teenagers? Have you formed any

stereotypes you need to re-examine? That all Christian kids are happy and well-adjusted, maybe? Many *are* happy, of course. But how have stereotypes interfered with your ministry?

Let's re-examine the attitudes outlined above.

EARLY EXPERIENCES

Avoiding young people because we were rejected in high school is to hide in a closet from which we should have long since emerged. We are acceptable because we are made in God's image and He loves us, not because we were popular at sixteen. Staying hidden in yesterday and acting out of early experiences prevents the healthy interchange between ourselves and our teens that might allow us to help when they need it now.

GOOD GUYS AND BAD GUYS

Putting youth in boxes keeps us from seeing them as they are — individuals with peculiar needs and ways of expressing themselves just like everyone else. They are not spin-offs of their progenitors the way the TV show "Rhoda" was of "The Mary Tyler Moore Show."

They are completely original creations signed by God, each different from the rest. Brother and sister, Joe is quiet and writes poetry to express his thoughts and vent his feelings; Sandy has strong opinions and lets everyone know what they are. Under stress, she jumps on her bike and pedals hard for miles; Joe finds a quiet, secluded spot and lays back, staring at the sky.

Whether quiet or obnoxious, the question to ask is, "Who is he or she underneath the surface?"

AIRHEADS

Kids *do* want to have fun. But then, so do adults. Not because we don't have a serious thought in our heads. Fun helps balance life. Viewing teens as "just crazy kids" keeps adults from taking them — and their problems — seriously.

A DIFFERENT BREED

They *do* need a world of their own because they are building an identity separate from that of their parents. But they still need parental acceptance and love as well as that of other adults in their world. Without it, they crumble.

FATHER KNOWS BEST

The show was cancelled a long time ago and so was the way of life it typified. Life now is not like it was then. Teens today live in families on the run who see each other only long enough to argue over who's going to use the bathroom first. Decisions may be over pot, smack or crack, not what to tell Mom about her pink sweater.

EXTENDED CHILDHOOD

See the teen years realistically. Youth are intense. They do dramatize things that happen. But the problems they deal with are heavy. *Shall I have sex? Have an abortion?*

Because many of them have parents that work, youth are left alone to do for themselves. And with erotica as available as penny candy was for their parents, the things they can choose to do are staggering.

NOT OUR RESPONSIBILITY

This one's reminiscent of the question Cain asked God and that has been echoing around the world ever since: "Am I my brother's keeper?"

We balk. *I am not the social conscience of the world.* True. Even Jesus Christ didn't try to be that.

But for whom are we responsible?

Just the children we birthed or adopted? Or others, too? What about the ones we pledged to help nurture and pray for when their parents brought them to the front of the church for dedication and we sat admiring their cuteness and laughed when they grabbed the minister's nose? What about the nieces and nephews on the other side of the country we seldom see? What about friends' teenagers — ones not related by blood, or perhaps not even part of our spiritual family?

We object, "I'll get in over my head. Do more harm than good. Injure my family in the process. Who knows what these kids could be like? Besides, I hardly have time enough for the things I have to do now."

God knows, objections like these are valid. We wouldn't know where to begin, which kids need our attention, which involvements are wise and which ones are not.

That's why we need to put God in charge of our friendships.

Years ago, I had no idea He wanted to be. Then, after a Bible study one evening, He pressed me to ask a young woman who was new in the group if she wanted to go to lunch that week. She had been quiet and somber all evening, but at the idea her face lit up.

That was the first of many weekly excursions for us. After several times together, she confided that she had been seriously depressed for months and was currently suicidal. Although she was seeing a counselor, she also needed friends who would accept and stay with her through her ordeal.

I had no idea things were so bad for her. We became friends and God gave us close rapport during her crisis months. From time to time, she struggled *hard* with suicidal feelings. She's much better now, and we're still friends, but she no longer needs the intensive support she once did.

That experience taught me that it's true — God does want to be in charge of my relationships. He knows when there is a wounded soul in my sphere of living — one I can help somehow. And it could well be a teenager.

DISCIPLED TO THINK ABOUT TEENAGERS

I've learned, though, that putting God in charge of my friendships means some radical changes. One is a shuffling of priorities. The time I've set aside for cleaning out a closet may have to be spent on the phone talking with a troubled youth instead.

It also means I must promote youth on my private scale of which people are important to me. *My friends, my peers, those with whom I have the most in common* were first. Youth rated several notches lower — different interests, different lifestyles.

The discipleship to which God calls us requires us to care about youth the way the Father does. That's not easy. I'm a long way from teenage myself and my own sons are well past those years as well. But, that's the attitude Jesus modeled.

Instead of associating exclusively with His peers, Jesus

was open to whomever the Father brought to Him — children, a rich young ruler, women, teachers of the law. He didn't stand in the synagogue aisle talking real estate with friends from the Chamber of Commerce. He gave His attention to the person who needed Him that moment.

To be discipled in God's attitudes toward youth would mean changing our preconceptions, moving the stakes that mark the boundaries of our lives, and in doing so risk rejection and take the initiative in building relationships.

The need to be open to the troubled youth in our lives was underscored in a conversation I had recently with someone who had grown up with an extremely low self-image and had been depressed. "The first person who helped me develop a measure of self-acceptance was my boss in my first job after high school," she told me. The *first* person? What about the others who had passed through her life until then?

There's another reason why a change of attitude is crucial. Our youth are the target of Satan and his demons, who are fighting in a last-days frenzy to gain followers. *Of all segments of society, our teens are probably the most vulnerable.*

McCandish Phillips writes, "Supernatural forces of destruction are now making swift headway in undermining . . . many of the nation's young people. . . . *The only thing that will break the grip of the supernatural power of Satan over young people today is the supernatural power of God.*"[1]

That power will not manifest itself in Sinai fashion with fire and billowy smoke and trembling earth, but through those in whom God is operative. We are the ones who have power in Jesus' name to destroy the works of the evil one.

BRINGING IT HOME

Ask God to disciple you in your attitudes toward the youth you know. In what ways do your attitudes differ from His? How can you better reflect His attitudes?

Have you ever asked God to be in charge of your friendships? If not, do so now.

What skills do you need to cultivate to build a relationship with a young person? Ask another Christian to whom you are close to help pinpoint them. Hold yourself accountable to that fellow Christian for developing these skills and relationships.

The Bakers' Story

Mr. Baker

Our son, David, was fourteen and a freshman in high school when he committed suicide. He did make what I call a feeble attempt to kill himself about six months before. We came back from somewhere and he had a rope as though he was trying to hang himself. My reaction was that he was demonstrating a need to get our attention in a threatening way.

At that time, David was having sessions with a psychiatrist, and we called the psychiatrist's office immediately, but were unable to reach him for several days. We filled him in and he took the attempt up with David, but we never got any adequate feedback except that the psychiatrist didn't feel it was a real effort.

Mrs. Baker

We talked with David about the attempt. He was not the type of kid whom you would tag as being depressed. He had a friendly personality, had friends in the neighborhood. But it's hard to tell about a fourteen-year-old. I would get conflicting reports about his popularity at school. I would go to one teacher and he would tell me everybody liked David while another teacher would give me mild negative comments.

Mr. Baker

He did have mood swings but generally they didn't last long. We know that David didn't have a good self-image. From time to time he would say, "I wish I were dead." We did not comprehend the full impact of his words.

Mrs. Baker

He got teased a lot. It is hard to judge just how much. He was small for his age. Despite the fact that he was fourteen, he had not started puberty yet. I think that boys who were maturing and were much larger were intimidating to him. His brother matured two years earlier. If that had happened to David, he might have felt differently. He would have been able to face things a little better.

Mr. Baker

He was going to a psychiatrist because he had been diagnosed by the school system as emotionally disturbed. We had taken him out of public school, put him in a parochial school, and they would not accept him unless he went into some sort of therapy. We thought he was making progress in that school, particularly in the last few months. He was much happier there. He started counseling in July, and he died the next February.

Mrs. Baker

In the sessions with his counselor, he heard all kinds of things he probably shouldn't have been exposed to. After a few visits he was put in with a group of children who were from divorced families, abused, neglected — ugly situations. We had a beautiful home life. We skied together, sailed together, did much together as well as having separate activities — and of course, went to church together. We enjoyed our children.

When people came to the funeral, they said they couldn't believe it. Over and over people said, "How it could have happened to a family like yours, we can't fathom." There were over seven hundred people at the funeral who waited several hours to talk with us after the service.

David's poor self-image was also due to his school situation. We didn't bring up our children to be modernists. I was opposed to sex education in the school after reading several curricula and discussing the subject with several pastors of different denominations. We tried to bring our kids up according to Christian principles using the Holy Bible as the standard of faith and practice. We are not ultra-conservative, but we're well-rounded people who get along with all kinds. We don't stay exclusively in our own special group although we are very active in our church.

We insist on certain values like honesty. Our children would go to school and see another value system entirely. I would shudder every time I went into the school and saw what I was putting them into. I got nowhere talking with his teachers in public school. They would insist that children must be exposed to everything and make their own decisions.

One time, our other son kept asking me what the Bible said about going to war, protesting and ending up in prison, that sort of thing. When I discovered that he was encountering these issues in public school, I read the books he was required to read and made arrangements to audit his classroom discussion. I was absolutely stunned as I listened to a teacher argue with this sixth grade accelerated class that it was courageous to protest and go to jail, that the Green Berets were vicious and that anyone who went to Vietnam and fought in that war was immoral. Those who went to Canada were heroes and we should reward them. The children knew better! I witnessed that personally. David was influenced by that type of attitude in his schools.

We would sit at the dinner table and discuss what was going on and how we felt about it. It was difficult for all three children, but I don't know what else you do. You raise a family and pray God will keep them safe and grant them the wisdom to deal with things like that. That was the kind of pressure David was under. We lived differently from our neighbors.

Mr. Baker

In Sunday school, they thought he was wonderful. People would say, "I wish our children were like him." People loved to have him in their homes.

David didn't want to go to the counseling sessions. I took him the week before he ended his life. I wouldn't say he was happy, but we had an excellent time together during that half-hour ride. We discussed the fact that he didn't want to go back to the counselor anymore. We talked about the fact that his schoolwork was improving, and that if it was as good as we thought, I would ask if we could stop the sessions. It was four or five days later that he committed suicide.

Mrs. Baker

I know I made mistakes, but I did the very best I could.

Mr. Baker

About a week before David died, we had a very bad snowstorm. I was responsible for making sure the snow was removed at the plant, so I decided to go there and took David with me. He met some of the men there on that occasion. A week later, when they heard he had committed suicide, they thought it must be another son. The little bit they saw of him made them certain it could not be that boy.

Mrs. Baker

I think something must have gone on that we have no idea about that just pushed him over. We don't have a clue as to what it was.

Mr. Baker

Drugs were not involved. The police evaluated the situation and told us that. There were drugs around where we lived and a fellow was obviously trying to encourage their use as well as some kind of pornography. About a month or two beforehand, David told us that. I reported it to the school.

He killed himself with a shotgun on February 16, 1978. I had one around for years with no ammunition; I never went hunting. I don't know why I kept it. It was in a cabinet out of the way. The Christmas before, we were invited to a hunting preserve to go target shooting. I bought some ammunition for that. David's brother and I went out to look for the preserve but couldn't find the place. We came back home, and I ended up keeping the ammunition.

Mrs. Baker

I have heard of many incidents, read extensively about the subject and suffered through many television programs on teen suicide — but nothing gives me any pattern of behavior or idea why David would do such a thing. I don't have any answers. One thing that has helped me to heal is the fact that I've faced David's suicide head on from the beginning. Of course, it must be noted that our pastor and church family were so thorough in their comfort and support, physically and spiritually, that God's power was released in us.

Our son knew he was loved. I have enormous comfort knowing that I loved my family, that they were at the top of my priority list under God. I don't know what else I could have done for our children.

Mr. Baker

One thing I wish we'd done is put him in a school a year later. That's hindsight, though. You don't really know it at the time, but he was young for his grade. Of course, a parent could run into the opposite problem, too: The child might be the first to mature.

Mrs. Baker

Yes, and I'd say get any child that is having difficulty out of the public schools. And another thing: I believe that unless true believers unite in *the* truth, use their gifts, become uncompromising with sin even in its more difficult forms, and pursue holiness, I don't believe there is much hope for the future.

7

RAISING HOPE-FILLED CHILDREN

One thing we can do is work to raise hope-filled children. "The real hope we have that's substantial and isn't going to leave us is represented in God's grace," counselor Bill Davis reminds us.

Not that a Christian world view, woven into the fabric of their lives, will repel dispiritedness like Scotchguard repels rain. Despite our best efforts, some will attempt suicide; some will succeed. But we can do our very best to provide a viable, alternative way of seeing the world — one that is plausible because it is based on truth they have not only heard and memorized, but assimilated and experienced personally.

To raise hope-filled children, we must be hope-filled ourselves. Rod Berg, a Youth for Christ director in Oregon, says "We've dipped through our economic doom and gloom, but it's still pretty heavy out there. There are still a lot of adults who don't have a lot of hope for the future . . . and it's going to rub off on our kids."

EARLY START

The ability to hope must be built at ground level, when

a child's perception of life is being formed and built of the kind of stuff that will withstand adolescent investigation.

Begin where God does, with faith based on creation. "For since the creation of the world God's invisible qualities — His eternal power and divine nature — have been clearly seen, being understood from what has been made" (Romans 1:20).

Junior Natural History Magazine founder Dorothy Edwards Shuttlesworth reminds us that "Children are natural explorers . . . If you are a wise parent, you will look upon these qualities in your child as a sacred fire — always to be fed, allowed to die out never."[1] An educated awe over creation can be an invaluable aid to hope.

That's where I turn when despair turns my insides sour. I go to the window. *Trees,* I think. *Drawing up nourishment, eating sunshine the way they were designed to do. And birds. Designed to soar and perch.* Knowledge about the natural world leads me to the creator. Slowly, the sun rises in my spirit. I embrace truth again. *You are good, I am convinced. I can trust You.*

KNOW WHAT'S HAPPENING INSIDE

Teach children more than Bible stories and verses to quote in drills and contests. Do raise them in an upbuilding Christ-centered church and a Christian environment. But do more than that. Talk with children about the spiritual information they take in. Let them tell you what they're thinking.

Six- to twelve-year-olds in one group were delighted when asked questions about the Bible stories they'd been taught. Adults hadn't been drawing them out and listening to them express themselves as they processed information.

One friend, a working mother, took a few minutes each evening to do that when her children were growing up by reading and discussing with them the stories in their Sunday school take-home papers and giving them a chance to talk about the previous week's lesson as they perceived it. To be successful, such times need to be more than a playback of mentally recorded facts, but a discussion of how the child perceives a God who let Joseph stay in prison or Paul be persecuted.

Knowledge about the Bible is invaluable. "Our whole basis of having confidence and boldness in living for God comes out of knowing that God's promises have been accurately written and preserved for us. . . ." says Hal Lindsey.[2] With family devotions bumped because of crowded schedules, each unit must find creative ways to work together with the church to teach truth. For some it is tucking in time, for others, dialogue about David and Goliath during after-dinner cleanup or while taking an evening walk.

Whatever way they choose, adults must do more with the Bible than feed promises like spoonfuls of strained spinach. They must facilitate the digestion and assimilation process and help youth take these first, shaky steps of faith. That means communicating a true understanding of what grace is all about. "Anything else is trumped up and goes away," counselor Bill Davis points out. "There isn't much in this world that's stable, that doesn't turn into something absurd very quickly.

"Too often young people can say the verses, follow the rules and look like Christians. But we can't turn them into walking, talking Christian dolls. They need to understand that Christianity isn't something we do to them, but something we introduce them to for their own consideration." That means, Davis says, learning to communicate to them on their own level.

That may mean getting better educated in spiritual subjects and the way we communicate them. One parent I know avoided Bible-related dialogue with her child. "She wants to know where God comes from — things like that. I don't know what to tell her. I just wish she'd quit asking."

I was just learning the answers myself when my sons were small. I had just become a Christian and we began together at ground level, children in the faith, poring over Bible story books, discovering Moses in the bulrushes. No need to push my way through years of theology to find the childhood within. No restlessness because I'd heard it all before. We were exploring and wondering together.

My boys are men now, but looking back, I wonder if perhaps that's not one of the secrets of raising hope-filled children. *Never to lose the wonder* that we are children of God blessed in the heavenly realms with every spiritual blessing in Christ.

SEE THEIR SEPARATE SELVES

I quickly learned as I mothered that these sons were

each unique individuals. One asked questions openly; another wondered silently. I needed to depend on the Holy Spirit to help me find my way into each child's mind.

It's the silent one who is easy to ignore, the mother of such a teen who made a suicide attempt told me, because the quiet one doesn't demand attention. "It was easy to leave her to her own resources when she was little." These children may be the ones who feel grief and stress most deeply and need more of our time so they can resolve it.

I also needed to learn a balance between integrating my sons into family life and allowing them to have an identity and an individual life. Worshipping, working and playing as a unit were vital but so was separateness. We learned the importance of excursions with each child — a burger with Dad, a walk in the woods with Mom.

For children do need to be separated from the pack and allowed to realize: *I am only myself. An individual with a right to choose differently from the family. And I have a parent who accepts me that way and wants to know that self without constantly picking at it, to fix it up, to make it over in his image.*

NO PERFECT PARENTS

Another important ingredient in raising hope-filled children is for parents to work out their own differences — and to get help if necessary. Otherwise, when Mama and Daddy explode angry words at one another, Junior may shiver under the covers imagining that it's his fault and feel his life sliding out from under him, the way some youth I know have done. No matter what, he must be assured that's not so and every effort must be made to show that such assurance isn't just empty words. (Don't burden children with knowledge meant for adults, though.)

"If the home is insecure, that's going to trickle down to the child in ways they can't put in words," one Christian therapist said. "That becomes one of the first reasons they panic or feel uncertain about their lives." If those experiences aren't acknowledged and discussed, they can rub a sore spot in a child's soul that grows deeper as he grows older.

A friend who had a long, troubled adolescence remembers when just such a thing happened to him. He was rifling through a drawer at home when he was about twelve years old. Curiously, he picked up and read an official-looking document. He gasped in horror as he began reading it. *Divorce.* That's what the paper said. "My parents had gotten divorced and they never told me." They had been separated. But a divorce? He cites that as one of the experiences that disillusioned him and sent him looking for courage on the streets and to near self-destruction through drugs.

Today's families provide less security than ever. They are broken into vari-shaped shards: single parents severed from mates by divorce decree; parents who are unwed; working mothers and weekend fathers; the extended family, scattered over thousands of miles with Grandpa in New Jersey and Grandson in Idaho.

Fathers, writes Leontine Young in *The Fractured Family,* have been largely phased out of modern life.[3] Divorce moves many of them out into bachelor apartments. Jobs become more sedentary so Father spends more free time on the racquetball court keeping in shape. In the time that's left, he must get the water out of the basement or moles out of the yard. Once the priest of the family presiding over evening Bible readings and family prayers, now he slumps in the family room staring at the ballgame on TV, too tired to talk or play or listen.

Rod Berg elaborates on this assessment: "This modern version of family is a stripped-down model of its predecessor when aunts, uncles, cousins and grandparents lived close enough to gather every Sunday for dinner. No more Grandma across the street and Aunt and Uncle across town. When the extended family stayed near one another, if Mom got real busy, then Son or Daughter could run to Grandma's *because Grandma was home.*"

Berg, a father as well as a youth worker whose work week extends far beyond forty hours, says, "My daughter just got a job at a supermarket and she works from 4 to 9 P.M. Usually we have dinner at 6, and she's not there a lot anymore. So we've got to make time to be available when she gets home after school or home from work so we have some time together."

Parenting by appointment may not fit our fantasy image of family togetherness, but it is a viable answer to today's problem. "I can't help you build a birdhouse now, but let's make a date for this evening after dinner." It is by making a

date to build a birdhouse and talking casually in the process
that we are able to help our youth interpret everyday life in
the light of truth and point them toward hope.

EXTENDED FAMILY

The job of raising hope-filled children doesn't belong
to parents alone. It's the job of extended family as well. Just
because aunts, uncles and grandparents are scattered geographi-
cally doesn't mean they no longer play a role in the process.

Only in recent years has the family been redefined as
a nuclear unit. In earlier eras when life was more rural, the
word "family" had a broader meaning — the one which is now
number three in the dictionary: "A group of people related by
blood or marriage: relatives."[4] *That is still the real meaning
of family.* Cousin Ben's three offspring in Yakima, Washington,
are one part of the people on earth with whom I am connected.
That's true even though distance may have stretched the relationship to a mere thread and difference in lifestyle or opinions
may have left us only nodding acquaintances.

Perhaps, though, you think of your kin as a series of
isolated cells unattached to one another. Ask yourself:

- Do I automatically exclude children in my extended family because of distance?
- Do I suppose that I cannot influence the youth
in my extended family toward Christian optimism
because there is no closeness between us now?
- Do I think of certain family members and go
back in my mind to disagreements that took place
years ago? Do I think, "Things have never been
the same between us since," and dismiss their prog-
eny from my mind?
- Do I suppose they wouldn't be interested in me
because I am older and live a different lifestyle?
- Do I find myself afraid to initiate friendship between us?

During your youth, was there one member of your
extended family who influenced you positively? Who? How?

The distant relatives may not be the only ones we have
tuned out. We may have also lost a sense of kinship with
young brothers and sisters. "We haven't anything in common.
Besides, I've been too busy getting my career going."

We go away to college and on to a job in another state and they're still at home. We begin families of our own and our connectedness to our own clan loosens until the ties hardly seem to exist at all. At weddings or funerals or on vacation trips, we come together and may sense belongingness. We may even make promises to "keep in touch." But back home, we get busy because the job takes more of our time and we have no more knowledge of their interior life than that of a mere acquaintance and little chance to help them hope.

If we look but do not see these who share our blood, we will probably fail to see that they could be one of the seriously depressed ones for whom life is losing its sheen. "But she's only a kid," we object.

Right. And kids are the ones who are in trouble these days. The current teenage crisis demands that we see ourselves as part of more than the nuclear unit. It demands that we see that the extended family is *real* family. They are persons to whom we *are* connected.

It's easier to tighten connections with young relatives across town or in the next city than with those far away. For relations close by, we can start with a dinner date and an apology for ignoring them. After that, we can keep in touch. Attend their baseball games occasionally, even if you're not a fan and freckle in the sun. That nephew playing third base may be lying awake nights wondering who he can tell about how badly he feels.

It's hard to cultivate intimacy with nieces and nephews and grandchildren who live a significant distance away. But when we take seriously youth's current crisis and God's urging, we'll find ways to try.

Modern technology provides ample opportunities to establish long-distance contact. Letters work for some, but regular phone calls when the rates are low, work for more. Subscribe to their hometown paper. Ask to receive the school paper. Become knowledgeable about that in which they're interested.

Nothing accomplishes as much as a personal visit, though, if the time is right. Try cutting back on luxury spending and save the money for airfare for them to come see you or for you to go see them.

If you aren't sure how to begin to get close to a child

in the family, try role-playing. Pretend you are fourteen years old. What could your aunt do that would link you two together?

Go slow. You may have nieces and nephews by the dozens and feel overwhelmed at the idea of establishing contact with all of them. Let God guide as to who should be first and how to begin. Don't overwhelm them. Let your easy, natural manner say, "I care."

Go easy on yourself, too. No guilt trips over things undone in the past. Start fresh and cultivate openheartedness to God for things He will do through you from now on.

Use wisdom. No hard-fisted sermons to make up for lost time. The object isn't to "get them saved." It's to be a friend to whom they can talk openly, as well as to "Always be prepared to give an answer to everyone who asks you to give a reason for the hope that you have. But do this with gentleness and respect" (1 Peter 3:15, 16).

Avoid earning a tag as a meddlesome relative counter-manding parental wishes. That will cast you as the bad guy and push you out of the family scene fast. Use tact and spiritual wisdom.

Initiate. They may *never* write you or call you back. Their parents may seem disinterested. The teen may seem not to care or may turn away when he enters various growth stages. Still, you can persist. *I care about you. I am interested in you as a separate member of the family. I want to know you as a person. I am here for you.*

Then if one of the units in our extended family is split by divorce, we will have a connectedness that allows us to help the children involved. Their parents may seem bitter or depressed, barely able to survive themselves and only intermit-tently able to assure their offspring that life will be good again. However meager our influence may seem, it *can* have a positive impact.

BRINGING IT HOME

What are some ways you can help develop hope-filled children? As a parent? Member of an extended family? As a neighbor? Church-goer?

Do you need to recapture the wonder of life? Go for a walk several times this week and look for special kinds of creation that are awesome. Talk to God about them.

Do you know a youth whose home life is insecure right now? What's one thing you can do to help him through?

8

BUILDING SELF-WORTH
AND COMMUNICATION

Since the passage from childhood to adulthood is one of the toughest any human can make — especially in modern society — it's no wonder the adolescent needs the understanding and wise support of parents and extended family to help him through.

Tom shares his experiences during those years:

"I was pretty happy until I hit high school. Then we moved. The kids in the new school were cliquish and I didn't fit. I wasn't a jock, I was just a skinny and sickly guy who went around carrying an armload of thick books. I became more and more depressed.

"My parents didn't make me feel any better when they kept telling me, 'These are the best years of your life.' *The best years of my life?* I kept thinking. If this was the best life was going to get, I didn't see how I had anything to look forward to. But my parents didn't understand.

"To add to my problem, I had to take medication for health problems and I didn't realize there was a side effect of depressive feelings. So the medication plus my experience in school kept me feeling miserable.

"I kept thinking about committing suicide. The only reason I didn't do it was that I couldn't figure out a painless way. My parents didn't have any sleeping pills and I sure didn't want to botch the job and wake up drooling, strapped to a bed.

"A friend and I used to joke that we couldn't commit suicide because there was no bridge in town to jump from. I smoked pot for several years as an escape.

"Then, after high school, three things happened that helped me get squared away. A reduced dosage of the medication I was taking pretty much eliminated the side effects. I met the girl who later was to become my wife. She accepted me as a person and that was the first time since fourth grade anyone had done that. And it was about that time that I invited Jesus Christ into my life."

LIKING THEMSELVES

Like many suicide-prone teens, Tom pinpoints an acute lack of self-esteem as one of the causative factors in his self-destructive feelings. Most of us recall our insecurity during those years. Like Tom, we ached for acceptance by our peers and cringed if it wasn't forthcoming.

If we perceive ourselves as losers, psychologist Emerey Nester points out, any further loss that comes our way only heightens our conviction that *we are losers* — whether it's elimination from the team, failure to be invited to the party or inability to measure up to parents' expectations.

"Most adolescents recognize not only a real self but also an ideal self — the person they would like to be. There is almost always some discrepancy between the two perceptions. In general, the larger the discrepancy, the greater the tension and the more serious the emotional malady."[1]

For me, the ideal was a girl in my class by whom I measured myself. She sang with a band, had a large following of friends, and laughed a lot. It took long, painful years before I realized that I could write, not sing; was happy with a few intimate friends; and was less gregarious than she. I was acceptable for who I was.

Listen to some of the things that made one group of teens I interviewed feel like losers:

"You let yourself down in your grades or in your relationship with God. You can't live up to what you think you should."

"I set goals too high and can't reach them."

"I have an older brother and my parents expect me to be like him."

"You do one thing wrong and then they never trust you again."

"Your parents tell you you're not doing your best and you know you can't do any better."

One thing teens desperately need from family is help in developing a healthy sense of who they are. But we can't present to them a positive self-image wrapped neatly and topped with a bow on their thirteenth birthday. From their early years, our words and attitudes have to imply, "You are a worthwhile, acceptable person."

But the brand of Christianity that some youth are taught is one long accusation instead of an affirmation. Finger-shaking, Bible-thumping adults may be well-intended, but can turn the way of Christ into a pharisaical code that reinforces guilt and worthlessness instead of teaching forgiveness, grace, mercy and hope.

Adolescents' intense yearning for peer approval — for the "in" crowd to give them the nod — is obvious to any observer. And the phenomenon has increased in intensity these last decades. In an interview with psychiatrist Warren Garitano, journalist Mary Ann Bendel points out that as recently as the 1930s there wasn't even a word in our vocabulary for people who are now called "teenagers."

Garitano responds: "Teenagers became a kind of independent sub-class during that period when there were great numbers of them. They began creating a culture that took its cues more from each other than from the adult world."[2] During their quest for personhood, acceptance by that much-publicized subculture becomes an all-consuming goal for most.

Parents and extended family can ease the struggle for self acceptance by consistently using every method available to teach children from their earliest years two things:

Who they really are.

How to cultivate a personhood in which they can feel at home.

THE REAL THING

"It's important to realize that we're not to build youth's self-esteem by pumping up and bootstrapping them into thinking they're great people," says professional counselor Bill Davis. "A genuine, positive self-image comes from the God who gave us a self. In a Christian setting, from the time they are small through the years when bodily and emotional changes make them uncomfortable with themselves, our words and attitudes must imply, 'You are worthwhile because God created you in His image and He accepts and loves you.' " God assures us of His love and acceptance in such Scriptures as these:

● "As the Father has loved me, so have I loved you . . . Greater love has no one than this, that one lay down his life for his friends" (John 15:9,13).

● "God has poured out his love into our hearts by the Holy Spirit, whom he has given us"(Romans 5:5).

● "For he chose us in him before the creation of the world to be holy and blameless in his sight. In love he predestined us to be adopted as his sons through Jesus Christ, in accordance with his pleasure and will"(Ephesians 1:4,5).

● "How great is the love the Father has lavished on us, that we should be called children of God! And that is what we are!"(1 John 3:1).

My own teenage years were one long quest for acceptance. I was middle-aged before I really believed God loved me.

Christian teens may have *heard* that message, but, like me, they may have failed to believe it. Instead, many have hung a caricature of themselves — a false portrait — in the back of their minds the way Tom and I did. *A reject. A loser.* Some may become self-destructive. Others, like Tom, consider suicide — especially when significant other factors are involved.

What then? How to change an unhealthy self-image into a healthy one? It's hard to get through to teenagers that they have worth. But it *is* possible. One teenager who felt worthless because his parents abandoned him began to change his self-concept when he became a Christian. He sat in our living room with amazement spreading across his face. "I'm really somebody. I never felt that way before. It's too good to be true."

To change a largely negative self-concept, he had to do as Nester says and "have experiences that contrast with how we presently see ourselves." So youth must experience continual acceptance by Christians and the cultivation of personal skills.[3]

REINFORCED SUCCESSES

Cathy Benitez, a child therapist who works with troubled youth in the Adolescent Care Unit of the Oregon State Hospital, spends much of her time helping them change the way they think about themselves. One way she does that is to pick out something in which the individual can have small successes. "Play a simple game with them — one they can win. If they like to draw, give them an opportunity to do so and approve their work.

"Go on to bigger projects. Try putting them on a behavior modification program to earn so many points. When they do, they earn a reward such as going swimming if that's something they enjoy. But start out with small things and build up to bigger ones so they can feel good about themselves.

"If a youth is depressed, he doesn't usually have the kind of energy necessary to be involved in something like sports. Work instead for small, individual successes such as playing a musical instrument." From their earliest childhood, children need to achieve, particularly in areas where they have special abilities. This affirms, *I am a person who is capable. I can't do everything well, but I can do some things. It's true — God has created me with special abilities.*

Families are the ones who can help children do that. Encourage them to pursue healthy interests, even if it's bug collecting when Dad had his heart set on his child learning to box. The extended family can pitch in, too, teaching children photography or bird watching or helping to cultivate other interests. Relatives living at a distance may not be able to cultivate skills directly, but they can be supportive by showing they are keeping abreast of a youth's important achievements, calling or writing to commend them and asking questions that show they are really informed.

LOVING REMINDERS

Always, it's imperative to affirm their worth, whether they succeed or fail: "I accept and love you because of who you are, not what you do." Psychologist Richard F. Formica puts it this way: "Really good loving takes place when a parent can see a child for what he is, accept him and enjoy him."[4]

One way we found to say "I love you because you're you" while our own three sons were growing up was by giving "Unbirthday Parties." On a Saturday morning, for instance, one of us would suggest a party for a family member — not to celebrate his birthday or some achievement but just because he was important to us.

Each of us lettered signs and taped them around the house. I fixed a favorite meal and together we prepared a "surprise box" — a cardboard carton stuffed with newspaper and small, inexpensive gifts.

These parties (thought up by my husband) were an unorthodox way to communicate caring with no strings attached. Letting your child know that you love and care about him is one of the most important steps to avoid a self-destructive attitude.

Read Ephesians 1:1-18 carefully and note as many reasons as you can why we are persons of worth. How can you make conversations with young people you know more upbuilding, instilling in them a genuine sense of self-esteem without preaching or seeming phoney? What kinds of opportunities do you have to help them cultivate skills or affirm those skills?

LEARNING TWO-TALK

"The most important thing to do as I see it is to build up a youth's self-image and keep open a line of communication so he can talk to you," Cathy Benitez says.

But one teen told me: "You can't talk to parents, can't tell them how things really are because they freak out when you do. I don't talk to my mother about anything important. Never have." Another agreed. "I can talk to my mom about how to scramble an egg. But when it comes to something really important, I can't."

Benitez goes on: "You can't just say one day when the child is thirteen years old or so, 'Okay, we're all going to start talking' if you never have. You can still do that, but it's not going to be as easy as when they were younger." One boy she worked with had attempted suicide numerous times. He did it because his home life was so unbearable and this was his way of calling for help.

Youth like these don't ask for help verbally, Benitez says, because they've never learned how. She suggests teaching communication by sitting down at mealtime at an early age and talking, letting them know "they can say whatever they want and they won't be condemned for it. Respect their opinions no matter what they are."

But how do you cope when their views could, if acted on, hurt them? Suppose the conversation turns to marijuana and the youth says, "I don't think smoking pot is harmful."

"Just keep talking," Benitez explains. "Say, 'Let's discuss it.' Ask what he knows about pot. Explain why it's harmful to the body and why using things harmful to one's body isn't right.

"Work hard at listening more and talking less. But you also have to be honest and tell them where you're coming from. I think families need to listen first and seek out guidance before they talk."

Bring up subjects you know they're thinking about. Like sex. That one was tough for me. I had to practice saying the proper names of body parts to myself so I wouldn't stumble over them in talking to my own sons. Still, it was tough to say "penis" out loud before males other than my husband, simply because I'd never done it before. But I persisted because I knew how vital it was.

TV provides all kinds of opportunities to talk openly about sex. A Gay Rights demonstration is flashed on the screen. Or a bedroom scene in the movie you've rented. A pro-abortionist speaks her mind. These can be springboards for casual conversation that allow teens to tell what they're thinking and for you to express your views in a friendly manner. Times like these work together to build in the mind of the youth a personal body of truth.

"No one else would ever listen to me before without telling me 'You can't do that!' " one teenager told a counselor I know. The counselor went on: "I can listen to kids tell me things that, if my own teenagers told me, would give me knots in my stomach."

Counselors do more than listen, of course. And parents must, too. But they must listen first and do it with understanding.

The word "understanding" literally means "to stand under or among." It denotes the ability to perceive — to comprehend — the meaning of someone's words. To hear not only what they say, but what they intimate.

"You'd be better off if I weren't here to cause you problems," may mean "I'm afraid you hate me, are sick of me and the trouble I've caused. If you reject me, too, I'd just as soon be dead."

Talk together about life on the inside of the self as well as on the outside. A common factor in suicidal youth is the inability to communicate effectively with the adults closest to them.

Dialogue about ideas. Youth are forming personal morality, weighing your values against those of peers and others, examining priorities, contemplating pieces of the world they're entering and studying them closely. If you don't maintain an open exchange with them, perhaps they'll hear only those with opposing points of view.

"Young people are inundated with information. They have so many choices," a therapist on a radio talk show about troubled youth pointed out. "Many parents fail kids because they don't help them sort out data and form some value systems." Which subjects do they find most troublesome? Use dialogue to hear what they're thinking and to offer your own reflections without preaching.

Dialogue about feelings. "How can we help a child to know his feelings? We can do so by serving as a mirror to his emotions . . . the function of an emotional mirror is to reflect feelings as they are, without distortion."[5] So reflect back a youth's feelings to him to help him see them clearly. Only then will we be able to emphasize the fact that Christians *do* have depressive, angry feelings even though we may not be used to talking about feelings at all.

"We get the idea that Christians never feel this way," one woman told me lately. But Bible writers, including David, certainly did. "All my bones are out of joint. My heart has turned to wax," he wrote in Psalm 22. Admit that you have felt depressed, lonely, misunderstood and angry yourself and that such feelings are normal for human beings.

Dialogue about personal experiences. It's our response when our teens share with us casual daily events that determines whether they'll go on to tell about their more deeply felt experiences. Accept each as a sacred trust. "They need to know they can tell me their worst thing and I won't fall off my chair," a counselor told me about his clients.

Dialogue about death. Psychiatrist Mary Giffin, who has specialized in the treatment of youth, says, "Often the child seems to believe that after death he or she will remain behind, gloating over the parents' grief. Perhaps because their lives have just begun, they cannot really conceive of finality."[6] One reason, she says, may be because the extended family is scattered and children don't have an opportunity to learn about death through personal experience the way they used to. Psychiatrist Warren Garitano adds that the ability to think in terms of real time is something that is only in a developmental stage in teenagers.

Use natural opportunities to talk about death. Always ask, "How does this make you feel?" Present it from a biblical perspective, building on previous conversations, giving more information as the child is able to understand and is able to receive it.

Sometimes, parents avoid dialogue because they are afraid it will lead to conflict. Issues that come up between parent and child can trigger something unresolved in the parent's life, counselor Jane Wolf points out. It could be because the parent is a conflict-avoider or because the present stirs up the past. In that case, "Parents have to get counseling for themselves. As much as anything, they need to understand their own issues. In some cases, they need to understand that the child has some problem; in others, that they are overreacting or underreacting to a situation based on some of their own problems."

What things are hard for you to talk about? Feelings? Dreams you'd like to fulfill? Experiences in which you did not excel? Choose one of them and talk or write about it to a young person soon.

Can you two-talk or is your conversation a monologue? Ask someone who loves you to help you learn to listen and remind you when you start to take over the conversation again. Work toward becoming more sensitive to the youth in your life who hesitate to talk to adults because adults never listen and don't understand. Think of one way you can begin to do that.

Listen to what they don't say. In an early scene in the

TV film, "Silence of the Heart," Skip, a teenager, stands in the kitchen with his mom. He's just found out that he's done poorly in his SAT tests. The girl he's crazy about doesn't want to go out with him.

He wants to tell his mother about it and about how devastated he feels. He starts to speak. But she's busy making food for a barbecue that evening. Later, he tries to talk with his father. Neither parent really sees the expression on his face, or hears his halting beginnings at conversation. Later, they realized they had been too busy to listen to the hints he gave that he was in trouble.

Skip represents teenagers who find it almost impossible to speak straightforwardly with their parents and other adults who are significant in their lives. So he lies to them about the SATs, doesn't tell them he's quit his job. He's afraid to be honest because he feels he isn't successful like the rest of the family, and is afraid they won't accept him.

Finally, Skip drives his car off a cliff to his death.

BRINGING IT HOME

Self-esteem and communication, the top two. Ask yourself: What can I do today to build a healthy sense of worth in my child? In a child who is a member of my extended family? How can I turn that action into a repetitive one? In what areas of communication am I most weak? What's one way I can get better?

9

HELPING TEENS COPE WITH LIFE

When asked in a TV interview about the popularity of the science fiction show in which he starred, a popular Hollywood actor answered that fans love the idea that the show portrays: that there will be a future.

It's tough to believe in the future when the world is falling apart, but it's tougher to believe when *your* world is falling apart — when Mom has moved out or Dad has moved in with another woman. It's tough when adults panic because family finances are as unsteady as beach sand and there's no "happily ever after," no neat, white-picket-fence home life like a child imagines others must have.

It can be tough for the so-called intact family, too, because something's gone wrong behind closed doors. Most of us assume that while church families may have problems, they would never perform unthinkable acts like child abuse and incest. But a mother who was abused herself as a child may be behaving the same way toward her offspring because it's what she knows. A father may be molesting his daughter and warning her not to tell. Spending Sunday morning from 11 to 12 in a church pew or in the choir loft is not inoculation against such acts. If the problem at home is you, get help fast. If it's someone you know, get help for them fast. Children who are abused often turn their desperate feelings inward on themselves.

Or perhaps the problem is that a family is upwardly mobile. "At first, we took the family with us when we moved, its traditions, obligations and permanence," writes Leontine Young in *The Fractured Family*. "Then, as we moved faster and faster, we began to drop off the excess baggage that slowed us down. . . . Families need a heart — that one person who provides the home base for everyone, who knows where everyone is and how everyone is getting along."[1]

Many of today's families are operating without a heart. They won't be able to find their rootedness and stability in "the old homestead where I was born and from which I left to get married." Nor are they part of a "Father Knows Best" unit with Mom in the kitchen baking cookies and Dad in the living room reading his paper.

BUILD STABILITY AND ROOTS

The family unit and lifestyle is changing and the source of rootedness needs to change with it. Not that having two parents isn't important. We do need to do all we can to preserve our marriages. And a sense of place is important, too. But most important is an internal sense of belongingness that remains even when externals change.

For stability is a fixedness of position and rootedness is settledness. And those qualities come from knowing *God is in control*. "We have this hope as an anchor for the soul, firm and secure" (Hebrews 6:19).

At its heart, stability and rootedness come from knowing *we are living in a triad. You, me and God*. A sense of security intimated by one's own inner settledness. Without words, that calmness implies that *we are safe because we live in the presence of God. We belong to Him. He will care for us.*

For youth born in an era of insecurity, it is spiritual rootedness, most of all, that enables them to stay planted like a tree by streams of water. We, their elders, can project that.

My husband and I had to learn to demonstrate rootedness and stability in a tangible way even though, as home missionaries, we moved every few years, money was tight and extended family were thousands of miles away. Sensing our closeness as a unit and our rootedness in Christ was vital to our family's well-being. One way we did that was by instituting family night.

We (including the children) took turns being in charge. The leader was given a small amount of money to spend and could divide it up between refreshments, game supplies and prizes. We ended the evening the way we ended most evenings — with family devotions.

Major in relationships. The clerk in a bookstore I visited, who had been experiencing turmoil with her daughter, put it succinctly. "We know what it means to establish relationships with other people, but somehow that gets changed when it applies to our children."

It shouldn't. For just as with non-related persons, our goal with the family's children is to deepen those close connections so they'll become enduring friendships.

Psychologist Bruce Narramore points out that "If we have been parents at the expense of being friends — it is time to make the change." By doing so, "We build an affectionate bond that makes them want to listen and to value what we say."[2] And we *can* be friends with a child, because a friend is simply "a person whom one knows well and is fond of."

Set boundaries. While they need our friendship, they also need us to set boundaries. Counselor Bill Davis points out that a lack of reference point to come back to when they're in the experimental stage can be frightening. Not having such boundaries can cause a tremendous amount of disorientation and a whole raft of symptoms including depression. He says, "To a young person who can hardly figure out who he is, that can accelerate and multiply his lack of security and contribute toward a depression that could end in suicide."

Boundaries need to be broad enough to allow growing room so children can make individual decisions based on Christian values, not secularistic existential ones. And boundaries should be understood, agreed upon and kept by all family members.

In addition, youth have to be free to examine the family/church's moral code. For only in doing so can they finally accept it for themselves. In a family where such discussion or where strong emotional statements ("I think that Bible

stuff is stupid!") are taboo, rebellion will probably go under-
ground and rise in some less desirable form. Whether or not
we like it, our young people are separate human beings who
must form their own values.

Doreen described her family as "quite religious." She
felt that they didn't allow her to make choices herself, the way
she needed to as she was growing up. When she had an
opportunity to go to a young people's conference out of town,
for example, they forbade it. She didn't feel free to tell them
how she felt.

Conflicts at home became worse and worse, and at
sixteen, her parents told her she couldn't see the boy she'd
been going out with. She swallowed pills. "I guess it was
about the only thing I could do so that they couldn't control
my life at that point — other than to leave. So I was really
showing them. It's sort of stupid."[3]

Model appropriate ways to solve problems. Children
don't *know* how to deal with stress. It isn't inborn, like the
ability to suck. For one disturbed young person I know, the
answer was alcohol. Why not? That's how her parents calmed
down. Others choose pills, just like Mom or a friend or their
favorite rock star. Or perhaps they learn to explode with violence
from parents who yell and scream and slam the door behind
them on the way out.

When we act self-destructively, we are playing and
replaying the act as a way to handle tension. A youth who
learns violence may finally turn that violence inward — on
himself.

Family therapist Ruth McEwen says that families who
play games by passing decisions back and forth because they're
unable to agree don't teach children how to make decisions.
"The young person figures he can play games with God. 'If
I pray just right, what I ask will be His will and I'll get it.'
This can only lead to frustration and deterioration of the young
person's faith."

My own mother seemed swamped with problems most
of my growing up years. When I became an adult and trouble
knocked the wind out of me, automatically I did what she'd
done — read my Bible.

I knew almost nothing about the Book and didn't know
God personally. But I knew it had worked for her. She never

preached about it but even after she died, I remembered.

Communicate wisdom wisely. Every parent is sure he has advice sound enough to be included in an updated version of Proverbs. Julie says: "Every time my parents talk to me, it's to criticize. They don't like anything I do. I'm never good enough. In between, we don't have much to say to each other."[4]

Our wisdom *may* be first rate because, through experience and thoughtful, prayerful meditation, we've gained insight in how to see from God's point of view. But Solomon himself couldn't have communicated wisdom successfully unless he did it under the guidance of the Spirit of God, dispensing it with tact and love and an understanding of the other person's place.

That's what Solomon did. Although he warned and exhorted, he did it kindly and always he repeated two key words — *my son* — words that emphasized a loving relationship. "Listen, my son, to your father's instruction" (Proverbs 1:8). No haranguing here. Instead, an unspoken "I love you. I am your father. I speak because I care. You are my son."

BE WILLING TO MAINTAIN ONE-SIDED RELATIONSHIPS

Sometimes it takes a double measure of patience to make it through the teen years. Patty had enjoyed a good relationship with her parents until the onset of adolescence. Now, her parents seemed so ordinary — not like the ones she fantasized they should be. Quiet and bookish, she felt awkward in social situations. Her parents were quiet people, too, and she blamed them for her lack of social skills.

Patty's parents sensed her depression and loneliness but didn't know what to do. Instinctively, though, they did do one thing right. "No matter how uncommunicative she was from time to time, we kept trying to draw her out," her father recalls. "Not by coming on too strong — that would have driven her further away. But by continuing to be her friend.

"We expressed interest in the things she was interested in. We talked on a day-to-day basis, while still giving her room to think and grow as an individual.

"She came through that period OK. She's still quiet. She's an artist and expresses herself that way. It was hard during those years. Sometimes I wanted to shake her or yell at her to let us into her life more than she was. Sometimes we vowed to treat her the way she was treating us. But we always went back to our plan — giving friendship when she wasn't ready to give it back. It was worth it."

Be human . . . Christian parents seem to have a harder time than non-Christians accepting their own humanity as well as that of their children. "Sometimes, non-Christian parents seem to be able to wade through the teen years more easily than Christians," Jane Wolf says. "Non-Christians are able to look back on their own years and say, 'I made mistakes and I survived.' Christian parents tend to spiritualize it all, rather than allow their child to go through what are normal developmental stages. They hang all the problems on disobedience to God."

To be human means that we have limitations. We make mistakes, we grow weary, we feel and express our frustration — sometimes too loudly. To finally accept our own humanness and that of our youth can be freeing and can strengthen communication.

. . . and be there. Maybe not at the door after school with milk and cookies, but with an expression of love in a letter, in a tape-recorded message, in a phone call. Be there to listen and to root to victory, even if it means turning off the evening sitcom or refusing an opportunity to play tennis with a new business contact that could lead to a great sale.

Learn about their world. "When my daughter started playing rock music, I began to get worried. How should I respond? What I decided was to sit and listen to it from time to time with her, learning about the group, and what they looked like, and paying attention to the lyrics," a friend told me. "Then we'd talk about it. I knew others might not approve of my approach, but I still feel it's a good idea."

One pastor-father I know goes to the movies regularly with his son. Afterward, they go out for something to eat and talk about what they've seen, about the values the film is communicating.

A youth leader suggested, "Walk the corridors of their school. See what it feels like to live there." Volunteer when the school needs help. Read the magazines your youth are reading. Watch the TV shows they talk about. Learn about their world by getting involved with them.

Family a distance away can browse record stores to

see what's new, help out with the youth group in their own church to get a feel for the young person's world, watch an occasional video, and note how teens are dressing and styling their hair.

Allow them to experience the real world. "I see again and again that many teens know virtually nothing of living with discomfort, of living with pain," Jane Wolf says. "We're fed a line that life is easy and comfortable and if you're doing it right, it'll all be coming up roses.

"Teenage is when you discover that childhood is over . . . and it's 'welcome to the real world.' And if everyone around you tells you it should be roses without thorns, that it should be easy when it isn't for you, then it's easy to assume there must be something terribly wrong.

"I don't mean to say that life is a drag. I think it's a real challenge. But to say it's all going to fall into place effortlessly is not what I see life as being. Neither is it my understanding of what the Scriptures promise."

Be ready for their transition. The time must come when teens struggle to own their own faith. Until now, they've listened wide-eyed to Bible stories about David and Joseph and baby Jesus and sat next to you in the pew. Now they question.

Be ready for their hard questions. "But why did God tell Saul to kill babies in 1 Samuel?" You may be secretly terrified they'll wander so far from the faith they'll never find their way back. "Parents have to spend an awful lot of time on their knees. That's not very psychological, but that's what I really do think," Jane Wolf says.

Pray hard for them, in faith, because you know God loves them even more than you do. And you know, too, that they're His, not yours. And He's the best Father there is.

BRINGING IT HOME

What do you usually do when you have to deal with stress? Which things are helpful and which are destructive? What are you teaching youth about handling theirs? Ask your pastor or a church leader to recommend a book on stress management. Read it and find three stress management techniques to build into your life.

Think of one thing you can do to let a young person

know you want to be friends. Do it.

Read Proverbs 2-7. Find as many ways as you can to communicate wisdom wisely.

How do you come across to teens? As a human being who succeeds and fails just like them? Or do you only talk about spiritual successes and keep silent about failures? Think of a time when another Christian's willingness to show he was human helped you.

10

BEING
A GOOD NEIGHBOR

Family members can't do the job alone. And they wouldn't have to if we were taking Jesus' words literally and "loving our neighbors as ourselves."

But since the urbanization of America began, we've had trouble deciding who in the world our neighbor is. I certainly have.

But I only began to look for answers after we moved into the house in which we now live. About sixteen years ago on moving day, I sank down on the front lawn between trips to the U-Haul and surveyed our new neighborhood. It was a quiet one with well-kept houses. Across the street was a large house and yard, next door was a brown house with a yard that bordered our own. *New neighbors to get acquainted with,* I thought.

Several years later, I sat in the same yard pulling weeds and evaluating my position in the neighborhood. I had made friends with across the street and next door. But I'd met others, too, down the block and even across the intersection — people who lived in houses I couldn't see from my windows. I was glad to know them. *But they aren't really my neighbors.*

I sat back and frowned at myself. *Not really my neighbors?* Who were my neighbors, anyway? Only the people in geographical nearness to me?

I thought back to years in city apartments where the only people with whom I attempted to form friendships were those next door or across the hall. Unless the circumstances were unusual (we talked on the playground where we both took our children, or we met walking our dogs), all others in the elevators were strangers and stayed that way.

ANOTHER MEANING?

Now, though, I was a Christian. Had the definition of "neighbor" changed? A search for the meaning of the word in Scripture revealed that in the Old Testament the word "neighbor" comes from a word meaning "an associate" and is translated as "others," "anyone," and "friend" as well as "neighbor."

In the New Testament, the Greek word for "neighbor" means "fellow man," as in the parable of the Good Samaritan.

"And who is my neighbor?" an expert in the law asked Jesus. His answer:

> "A man was going down from Jerusalem to Jericho, when he fell into the hands of robbers. They stripped him of his clothes, beat him and went away, leaving him half dead. A priest happened to be going down the same road, and when he saw the man, he passed by on the other side. So, too, a Levite, when he came to the place and saw him, passed by on the other side. But a Samaritan, as he traveled, came where the man was; and when he saw him, he took pity on him. He went to him and bandaged his wounds, pouring on oil and wine. Then he put the man on his donkey, took him to an inn and took care of him. The next day, he took out two silver coins and gave them to the innkeeper. 'Look after him,' he said, 'and when I return, I will reimburse you for any extra expense you may have.'
>
> "Which of these three do you think was a neighbor to the man who fell into the hands of robbers?"
>
> The expert in the law replied, "The one who had mercy on him."
>
> Jesus told him, "Go and do likewise."

> Luke 10:29-37

Sociologists tell us that we set limits on whom we consider to be our neighbor. Rarely, they say, do we consider people across an intersection, for example, to be in that category. Houses must be in immediate proximity to our own, lawn to lawn, or they must face our own, so that we are a cluster of wood and brick siblings unseparated by ends of the block.

Reflections on the Samaritan parable convinced me that Jesus was redefining the definition. He pushed back all boundaries. Then they were national and religious. Now they are geographical and, perhaps, ethnic and economic. His definition demands that I tear down in my mind old concepts of who neighbors are and enlarge them as He did to include not just next door and across the street, but those in the area perhaps where I walk my dog or get my evening exercise.

But there are others, too — the ones, like the wounded man in the parable, with whom I "happen" to have contact throughout my day — from morning stretch to evening yawn. Not only upstairs or next door, but the group of fellow men who people my corner of the world. That includes the ones who are under eighteen who play their radios too loudly and run across my lawn.

TAKING RISKS

My mind balks. *Privacy. Making friends with people in your neighborhood can be bad news. They park in your living room and bend your ear. Besides, I'm too busy to have relationships with everyone who crosses my path. Anyway, I have problems enough of my own. I can't take on a bunch of kids who've probably made their own misery. Or their parents who may want me to commiserate with them about their kids' behavior.*

They never made a move toward me. What if I take the initiative and they just sit there? I'll keep to people who are safe, people I know — people like myself, thank you.

Sure. We *can* keep to people like ourselves. But if we do, we've cast ourselves as priests and Levites in the Samaritan parable. They were not the good guys.

If we were the expert in the Law who prompted Jesus to tell the story, we might ask Him another question. "What is my responsibility?" And Jesus would probably say that He'd answered that already.

So we'd examine the parable again, harder this time, the way He required disciples to do. This time we'd see:

The Samaritan looked at him, not through him.

Took time out of his carefully planned day.

Made the first move toward the wounded man.

Looked with sympathy.

Gave emergency care.

Took him to a place where he'd receive long-term help.

Provided money to pay for his recovery.

Christ's interpretation of the law replaces the limited edition version written and imprimatured by pharisees throughout the centuries. It mandates non-prejudicial, *agape* involvement with whomever God brings to our attention.

A MODERN VERSION

Imagine that the Samaritan story was about a severely depressed teenager instead of a stripped and beaten man left half dead. The boy was driving from the outskirts of town back to his home when he began to brood over Sally, the girl he'd gone steady with for nearly a year. "It's all over," she'd told him the night before.

Without her, he didn't know what he'd do. She made him laugh, made him feel good about himself. Mom and Dad didn't know yet. He hadn't told them. He didn't tell them much that was important. They were both always busy with the business or their bowling team. Lately, when they *were* home, they were either arguing or not speaking. So he'd spent most of his free time with Sally.

She never laughed at him because of his learning disability the way the other kids did. He needed her. But she'd gotten tired of being needed. Tired of him.

He slumped down behind the wheel. *What's the use? Nothin' at home. Nothin' at school. No college. Now no Sally.*

The pain inside was like a knife cutting away parts of his body. He'd hurt so bad so long. But this was more than he could take. *What if I slammed the pedal to the floor and took the car over the bank?*

Instead, he swerved into the parking lot of a fast-food restaurant. *Got to think. Got to decide.*

In a booth, he sat staring at his Coke, his eyes heavy-lidded and dull, his mouth drooping. Just staring.

Finally, he looked up. *Worse luck.* People from church at another booth. He'd forgotten this was a favorite stop for the adult church crowd. His Sunday school teacher and youth leader sat across from one another, talking and finishing off hamburgers. They both kept getting after him to participate in church activities more, to do more of the social things. But who felt like playing stupid games?

They'll see me here alone, looking miserable, and come over. But they got up, and headed past him toward the door, still talking to one another. He heard them say something about making more space for the primary department and needing more chairs. They did turn to look at him and say a quick "Hi" as they went by.

The boy made wet circles on the table top with his glass. *What's the use? Nobody cares. Why should they? I'm nobody important, anyway. A nothing. I don't deserve to live.*

That's when he heard a voice say, "Mind if I join you?" It was the guy who lived two doors down from him. A nice guy. Always wanted to know what was going on with him and took time to listen. They'd talked about school and about his learning disability. "You need someone to help you study? Let me know," he'd offered.

Of course, his neighbor knew about the arguments at home. With the windows open, he could hear most of them.

The two of them had planned on going fishing during the steelhead season. His parents discouraged their friendship, though. It seemed their neighbor and his family went to a church they didn't approve of.

"You look really down. Things not going so well?" The neighbor smiled and waited a moment. "I've had plenty of down times myself. Want to talk about it?"

The boy hesitated. Would his neighbor understand?

"I know things have been tough. Has something else happened?"

The boy had to take a chance. He had to tell *somebody.* "Yeah, something sure has . . ."

What has been your definition of "neighbor"? Has it included the youth in your immediate area? What do you know about the way they're thinking and feeling?

A friend and I were talking about youth suicide when he told me about an experience that brought the importance of involvement home to him. "It happened three years ago. She was fifteen years old. She lived a block and a half from me. And she killed herself.

"I went to the funeral and wept because of the loss. But I wept also because I kept asking myself, 'How come I didn't know she was in trouble?' Here she was, a block and a half away! How come I didn't discover it?

"I became good friends with her sister after the funeral. That's how I found out that the dead girl left a stack of poetry. The ones I read depicted constant loneliness. How come I didn't know?"

We do tend to look accusingly at ourselves when a tragedy happens near our front door. None of us knows whether this fifteen-year-old's suicide could have been averted. My friend might *not* have made a difference. And we certainly cannot take on the guilt for another person's self-destruction.

What we can do is commit ourselves to involvement in the lives of teenaged neighbors when the Spirit of God leads us to do so — networking with others to ease a youth's loneliness, to provide belongingness and hope. And networking with their parents to provide support.

Psychiatrist Donald Jackson experienced personally what he knew professionally — that it's vital for a teenager to have someone mature to talk with. Jackson's teenaged son had a quiet sixteen-year-old friend who spent time at their home. The doctor and the boy talked from time to time, but only casually, the way acquaintances do.

"As time passed, Jackson lost track of the gangly teenager, until one Christmas ten years later he opened a Christmas card and found a note from the former visitor. In the note, the young man, then in his late twenties, revealed that during the period he had visited the Jackson home, he had been so troubled that he had been thinking of killing himself. He said the reason he didn't was that in Jackson he had found someone who was open, interested in him, and willing to listen."[1]

NETWORKING

To understand the principle of networking, imagine a young patient admitted to a sprawling city hospital with a potentially fatal ailment. In charge of his treatment is his primary care physician, who calls on a network of other people in the institution skilled in various facets of the healing process to assist him. An x-ray technician takes blood, an anesthesiologist sedates the patient during surgery.

Others not part of the primary care unit also play a vital role: the clerk who takes information in admitting, the orderly who transports the patient from one unit to another, the aides who refill his water pitcher. Medical and non-medical personnel networking together.

The team does not save every patient. But to have the best chance, every staff person must show up for work equipped to do the best job possible.

It's essential that they not decide for themselves which patients they'll care for today and which ones they'll ignore. The patient's physician, not the individuals themselves, is in charge of the case.

The kingdom of God is like a hospital because its members are called to care for and treat the ill — especially in an epidemic like youth suicide. The neighbor principle is an integral part of the healing system. Like others in the network, each is to report daily to the physician in charge for directions. "What's my role today, Lord? To invite the boy who mows my lawn in for a Coke when he's done? Speak to the boy who walks home past my house every day — the one who's always alone and somber-looking? Please lead me to the vulnerable ones, the hurting, lonely youth. Help me to turn one of them into a friend."

Developing real intimacy — that inward, personal, experiential knowledge of a youth — is hard. Child therapist Cathy Benitez says, "Most adolescents feel pretty threatened by adults, as though you're trying to get inside their heads or playing games with them. It takes time to make them non-defensive until they feel comfortable talking with you."

That may require a different set of priorities from the ones we have now. But we're called to be neighbors. Jesus made that plain.

Neighbors reinforce young people's worth by acknowledging that they are alive and that we're glad they are part of our world. We must refuse to categorize them as less than friends. I realized how deadly the tag "neighbor" can be a few years ago. I was visiting someone who lived nearby when the phone rang. "Can I call you back? My neighbor is here." Then my hostess explained. "That was my friend Debby who lives on Adams Street." I felt a contrast she probably didn't intend — that I wasn't a friend. Only a neighbor. A second-class person in her life.

Although neighbors aren't primary-care people in the lives of teens, they can form relationships that will minister. The impact of their contribution is heightened if they are part of a team — a network — each communicating in their own way that "life is worth living."

GIVING THE MESSAGE

The message everyone in the network should ache most to give is the gospel of Jesus Christ. In what follows, two professional youth leaders — Morris Dirks, a successful youth pastor at a large Oregon church, and Rod Berg, a Campus Life staff leader — share their ideas about how to do so successfully.

Morris Dirks: "The adult who is sharing the gospel with a teenager must earn the right. He does so by being in touch with the teens' world and letting them know he cares. The old saying is true, 'Kids don't care how much you know until they know how much you care.' "

Rod Berg: "If a young person is struggling because of a friendship problem or a boyfriend just told her to take a hike or she's having parent problems, and you don't deal with that along with sharing the gospel, it isn't necessarily going to be the solution.

"In Campus Life, we share on four levels: physically, mentally, socially, spiritually. It allows the individual to know you care about the total person, that you're not merely interested in getting another notch in your belt and moving on to the next conversion."

Berg explains that the way to relate physically, mentally socially and spiritually to a youth depends on the talents and needs of the individuals involved. "You may have talent as a tutor and can sit down with this person and help him with a tough class. Another person may have talent as an athlete and can jog or throw the discus or play tennis. Or you may meet on a social basis and show some good times and make the youth feel warm and comfortable and have good conversation.

I feel strongly that kids need to know you're interested in their problems as well as their spirituality. Then you'll have the opportunity to share spiritually as you share their world."

Morris Dirks: "One thing we need to keep in mind is that teens have very strong felt needs. And we need to move toward their felt needs as the basis for sharing the gospel. So often, I think the place to start is not with the plan of salvation but with where the young person is in his life.

"We need to show him that God's Word has some answers for him regarding the opposite sex, peer pressure, parents and other potential problem areas. Share with him that the Bible is relevant to his needs. He'll begin to realize that the Bible has something to say to him about life in general. As kids begin to see the relevance of the Bible we can begin to help them understand the person of Jesus Christ. He is a personal friend who is very relevant to their lives. When they understand this, salvation begins to take on new interest and importance."

BRINGING IT HOME

Did you have a neighbor who made your own teenage easier? What did he or she do for you? If you didn't have such a person in your life, think retrospectively about things someone could have done that would have helped.

Which way could you best relate to a young person? Physically, mentally, socially or spiritually? Brainstorm specific things you could do in each category. What old behavior patterns keep you from doing them? Change by instituting a series of small steps toward your goal.

Find scriptural principles you could share with a youth who is having family problems, who wants friends, who feels like a failure.

A Youth Counselor Talks to Adults

Jim Taylor, Counselor, Hillcrest School

Jim Taylor has been a counselor at Hillcrest School of Oregon, a residence for youth who have committed a crime that, if they were adults, would send them to the penitentiary. The adolescents under his care are extreme examples of behavior described in this book.

All his time at Hillcrest has been spent counseling girls. Taylor says:

"Part of our program at Hillcrest is for every student who comes into group meetings to tell what we call 'a life story.' That includes things they have done in the past: when they've hurt themselves or someone else, had difficulty with the law or had family problems.

"I'd say probably 60 percent have talked about making some kind of suicidal gesture before they ever got to Hillcrest. Usually, it's cutting on their arms, wrists, or use of drugs. I understand from other counselors that boys generally try more violent things.

"I'd say that 100 percent of the girls I've had have been physically abused in some way. And probably 80 to 90 percent have been sexually abused. That was a real surprise to me. It took me three or four years to realize that the percentage was that high.

"Most of it happens within the family itself. That breaks down any kind of feeling of trust and confuses what love and trust and hate really are. So the girls direct the anger and hurt they feel toward themselves.

"What I've seen since I've been here is mostly suicidal gestures, like cutting on their arms. They say they do it because 'Nobody listens to me, nobody cares for me.' They feel like they're alone. Nobody wants them, nobody loves them. They direct the violence and anger they feel toward themselves.

"A little later on, when the crisis is over we say, 'You were responsible for what you did to yourself. There are other ways you can deal with your anger.' Some of the kids have tried pounding on their pillows or mattresses. But usually they say, 'That's not hard enough. It doesn't hurt enough.' If the pain and hurt isn't there, they don't feel like they've gotten the anger out. They tie anger with pain. And I think most of the time that's because of the kind of lives they lived or were stuck in before they got here.

"The way we deal with it is to deal with the behavior that's taking place at the time. If the girl has made cuts on her arms or, as the psychiatrist calls it, done 'delicate cutting,' we take it seriously. We make real efforts to observe them more closely, to not allow them to be isolated from people. We keep them out of their rooms where they can be all alone or out of other areas where they can segregate themselves and have an opportunity to do it again. We also take all the things out of their rooms we can find that they can to hurt themselves. Thumbtacks. Mirrors they can break. Things like that.

"The second thing we do is not give them a lot of mileage or attention over the behavior to reinforce it. I do emphasize the fact that it hurts me to see them injure themselves and that's why I'm doing everything I can to keep it from happening again.

"We contact the medical department so they can first of all take care of medical needs. Then we contact the psychiatrist.

"I don't believe we can make much of an inroad in teenage suicide so long as our society goes on advocating, teaching, promoting and allowing violence. Most people talk about violence on TV, and that's true, it does depict a lot of violence.

"But I don't think that's the only place the kids see violence promoted. In the political and economic scene, we are taught that the way toward peace is through violence. 'Let's be the strongest, the biggest

and the baddest and we'll have peace and everything
will be all right.' We are told that violence is the
way to solve problems.

"Is it any wonder that when kids are frustrated
enough, they take it out on other people or
themselves? When they feel hopeless enough, I don't
think they tend to direct it outward, but they direct
it inward. Whichever is the closest and easiest at
the time.

"I've heard over and over again from different
girls about parents fighting or arguing. The dad was
beating the mother or she was hitting him. Or a
father was beating another child and the girl
invariably says, although maybe not in these words:
'They're all angry and it's my fault. The family is
falling apart and it's my fault. Because every time
they get angry, they holler at me and send me to
my room. They beat me.' Then the girl directs it
inwardly. 'I'm no good. I'm guilty.'

"So, many of the girls connect love with pain.
If Satan can confuse the total issue of what love is
to the point where love and pain have to go together,
he can make people do all kinds of abnormal,
un-Christian things in the name of love, in the name
of 'I care.'

"I think if Satan can get people to 'sacrifice
themselves' through suicide or even to shed blood
for the wrong reason, in a spiritual sense his kingdom
is enhanced.

"The kingdom that Christ came to establish is
separate from the kingdom that Satan has. And it
ought to be different. It's clear to me that there's a
power in Christ's blood, shed for our sins."

11

THE CHURCH'S MINISTRY TO YOUTH

Seventeen-year-old Eddie had been coming to the youth group for several months, brought by a friend. Now, he sat bent over, his head in his hands. "It never gets any better," he told Sam Merrill, the youth pastor. "I'm tired of fighting this battle! I mean, what's the use? Life is the pits! I feel like I just want to quit."

Pastor Sam had learned that life at home for Eddie was unstable and family relationships very poor. It was no wonder the boy felt the way he did.

Sam Merrill worked hard to build a friendship with the youth and spent time talking with him about his feelings and the reasons for them. "Eddie called me often, just to talk," Sam recalls, "Sometimes, I felt I wasn't making any headway. But I kept challenging him, helping him see how he could work on some of these areas that were problems.

"There were crises when it looked like we were very close to a possible suicide. I'd go to check on him, to see how he was doing."

Gradually, Eddie's attitude began to change. From a very depressed person, he developed into one who was resolving some of his tensions, becoming comfortable with other people and even reaching out to them. It took time and Pastor Sam's patient perseverance, as well as the loving friendship of others in the group. "If the youth group hadn't been supportive — if it were clique-oriented, I'd be very concerned where Eddie would be now."

COMMUNITY

Eddie is doing well now largely because the local church embraced him and didn't let go. In Pastor Sam and the group's young people, he found the loving acceptance, the sense of hope and purpose he needed, to go on living. In an era when the family tree has been hacked down at the roots — its limbs splintered and scattered — it is urgent that the church be that kind of place for the Eddies of this world.

Youth like Eddie can find loving acceptance, an environment of hope and a philosophy that resounds with purpose in the church. Counselor Bill Davis points out: "Teens disconnect from their own parents but go seeking other significant adults like a coach or a youth director. If significant relationships happen in the Christian family, that person the teen seeks out could be a trusted Christian. Those relationships can be established in the church if we are living in community."

The word "community" comes from "common" or "shared by all or many."

The apostle Paul wrote about Christian community:

"In Christ we who are many form one body, and each member belongs to all the others" (Romans 12:5). "Now you are the body of Christ, and each one of you is a part of it" (1 Corinthians 12:27). Every member of the body is as valuable as every other. Because we *are* a body, we are interrelated, interdependent.

Pastor Ray Stedman says about the uniqueness of the body of Christ: "It is the sharing of life that makes a body different from an organization. An organization derives power from the association of individuals, but a body derives its power from the sharing of life."[1]

It is that life shared in Body ministry through relationships born out of community that can help save the lives of teens like Eddie.

But that can happen within the church structure only

if opportunities for adults to *be with* teens are built into the regular schedule.

One pastor told me, "The church is one place where we're transgenerational. But I think we need to work harder at bringing the two generations in contact with one another. Youth live in a peer-dominant world. They go to school together, socialize together, play sports together. Even in church, the two age groups often operate in segregation from one another — adults in their own classrooms and the teens in theirs."

Sitting together in the same pew during the same hour on Sunday and stopping for a word in the aisle on the way to the door just won't do. How to break down the generational barriers?

• Fun nights when everyone — children through adults — play together, stumbling and sweating or competing more quietly the way families used to do in front of the fireplace on long winter evenings.

• Picnics, eating watermelon and dripping juice on shirts, roasting marshmallows together to see who can get the one most perfectly browned. Not teens in their clusters and adults in theirs. Friendly, casual intermingling by adults who think young.

• Some churches, particularly larger ones, have instituted care groups within the church that provide opportunities for personal, intergenerational relationships. Called by a variety of names such as kinship groups, circles of concern, family groups and shepherding groups, they meet separately from the larger church to sing, sometimes to study Scripture, to share one another's needs, to pray for one another, to give the Holy Spirit an opportunity to work, and to commit themselves to be accountable to one another and be available throughout the week.

Betty Mitchell, founder and executive director of Good Samaritan Ministries in Portland, Oregon, believes adults and teenagers should have opportunities to be trained together as well. "It's like an army," she says. "If you put all the parts of the army in different kinds of training, when you put the army together, they're not going to be able to work together."

In her ministry, "We teach the whole family the same concepts. Then at least they have some common ground to build a house."

A church I attended several years ago performed just such an experiment. Departing from the traditional Wednesday evening adult Bible study, they instituted a potluck supper followed by the presentation of a simple scriptural concept. Then, those present broke into groups, each made up of individuals of all ages, and performed an activity that related to the principle.

Worshipping together, playing together and learning together in ways that fit each local body gives an adult the opportunity to get to know sixteen-year-old Sue as a sophomore who loves to play basketball and write poetry to express how she feels — not merely as Bev Bromfield's daughter.

"Most adults don't have the time, or won't make the time, to get acquainted with a teen," one pastor told me. "You can't just drop into a young person's life and drop out again." The answer, says youth worker Rod Berg, "is spelled T-I-M-E." Consistency. Dependability. Commitment to build a relationship with that young person to whom God leads you. And it takes more than the hours a youth spends in church to do it. The white building on the corner is just a place to drop into and get out of, not a place to get real in — unless adults change that image.

The testimony of one seventeen-year-old who had attempted suicide tells what can happen when Christians get involved. The boy stood in church and looked around at individuals in the congregation. "I couldn't have made it without you. It was your love, your caring, that got me through. You gave me something I never got at home."

EFFECTIVE YOUTH MINISTRIES

"In a youth group like ours with fifty or sixty kids, we may have a number who are suicidal," a youth pastor told me. The thing that will make a difference, he believes, is if students and staff reach out in love. Knowing someone really cares is an important way to change an individual's mind about suicide.

But it's only through a core group of Christians, both youth and staff, who have been discipled themselves — who are other-centered instead of self-centered — that life-saving can be done. One-to-one friendships established within the youth group, slowly and sometimes painfully cultivated (the way Sam did with Eddie) are the primary means by which despairing youth will find hope in the church. But the structure of the group itself — its goals and the philosophies that determine the activities provided — is also vitally important.

Effective youth ministries reach teens in the four major areas of their lives described in the previous chapter: physically, mentally, socially and spiritually. They do that through:

• Nine innings on the softball diamond.

• Gab sessions like the ones my husband led with teens in one of our churches. No subject was off limits. No ideas put down.

• Ski trips, rafting trips and the like. "The youth group isn't established to provide fun for its own sake — to appease or entertain the kids," Morris Dirk says. "But I feel fun times are critical because they allow teens to get away from the pressures of everyday life in an interlude. I find that when a depressed young person goes away to a setting like that, the cloud lifts. It's often at times like that, when the youth is relaxed, that relationships are built and the youth will open up and reveal a glimpse of his true self to the adult on the scene."

• Integration into your outside life. One youth pastor brought a teen with him when we met to do an interview for my research. Others take youth with them whenever they can to build a relationship — from breakfast before school to a trip to the town dump.

• The teaching of biblical concepts. Youth pastors I talked with emphasized that, although large group meetings are important, small group meetings are equally important. One church has instituted ICU's (Intensive Care Units), another Acceleration Groups. Both teach key principles relevant to a teen's life *now*, discuss them in small groups where exchange can take place, and provide opportunities to practice the principle in everyday life.

One hurting teen may open the door to his insides while panting on the sidelines next to the adult he just beat at volleyball. Another may do so in a small discussion group.

While church cannot substitute for home, effective youth ministries can provide . . .

• *A sense of belonging.* One counselor whose practice is limited to depressed people told me, "I've stuck my neck out with many parents and said, 'You need your kids in a

youth group that's moving — in a group to which the kids can
be proud to belong.'

"A teenager does need something to belong to that he's
proud of. Some youth groups are big and flashy and about all
they do is take a trip here and there and provide social activities.
If a young person is growing in a small-sized youth group,
fine. If not, find one that can provide what is needed," this
counselor suggested.

She has sometimes urged parents to take their teens
to meetings of a parachurch organization, such as Young Life,
Campus Life, or Student Venture, in addition to their own
youth group. "I've seen a change in these kids. They stay in
their church and meet when they have someone who'll meet
with them. But they have another group about which they can
say, 'This one's moving.' "

One young person said of such a group, "Coming here
has helped me a lot. I can talk out my problems in the group
and the leader has helped me, too."

● *A sense of continuity.* Teens today have little sense
of longevity the way youth did in earlier years — little connectedness with other generations. Because families are split and
mobile, the teenager, his parents, grandparents and other relatives are not likely to worship together regularly. A youth group
can help provide a sense of belongingness not meant to substitute
for family, but important nevertheless during those years.

● *A sense of acceptance.* Accept youth as they are.
That means jeans and t-shirts instead of shirts and ties. Long
hair, spiked hair, mohawk, whatever the current fad.

A young person contemplating suicidal thoughts may
feel like a misfit, a youth worker pointed out. At home, his
brothers and sisters make good grades and please his parents
but he can't. At school, he's not athletic. Maybe he was rejected
because the one good friend he had dropped him.

If the church and youth group set additional stringent
standards (demanding unrealistic, Christianized behavior, for
example) instead of letting youth be themselves (within limits,
of course) they will only discourage, not encourage, the youth.
Accept young people the way God Himself does — exactly as
they are. After all, He does the same for us.

● *A sense of purpose.* "Teens need to know what the
purpose of life is, just as adults do, and that's something with

which the church can help them," counselor Jane Wolf says. But she adds that the adults who teach them must first have the questions answered to their own satisfaction.

When Wolf teaches an adult Sunday school class, she sometimes asks students to write out their philosophy of life. She says that sometimes a student will remark that he was amazed he didn't know the answer. They'd been churchgoers for years.

Wolf also emphasizes the fact that youth need to understand that the world doesn't revolve around them, that it belongs to God and we are to revolve around Him and do His will.

HELP YOUTH EXPERIENCE A SENSE OF ACCOMPLISHMENT

Within the church. Are those crazy, inept kids too clumsy to get up on the platform, too bungling to be entrusted with any important part of the service? Maybe their voices *are* changing, and growth spurts *do* leave them uncoordinated. They may be half-child, half-adult, but still *they do need to feel contributive.*

To provide a significant sense of accomplishment, participation in church services needs to be more than the token annual "Youth Night" when teens are paraded out and shown off, then taken away for another year. Why must our worship services be smoothly orchestrated hours manned only by experienced adults who rarely miss a cue? Why not family worship which youth can lead in appropriate ways?

One Oregon church provides an opportunity for every young person to work with an adult in an area in which that teen is interested. One may assist the person who mans the sound system, another assists in the nursery, still another in a Sunday school class. There are a host of possibilities: an artistic teen can help teachers make visuals; one who likes to write can work with the editor of the church newsletter. Not only does this provide a sense of accomplishment, but working with a mature Christian also provides a valuable opportunity to establish a relationship. (And hopefully motivates the adult to keep his life in good spiritual shape.)

In community service. "Put teens to work," Bill Davis urges. "Provide opportunities for them to help in homes of the elderly, for example, in ways where they make a significant

contribution and can see tangible results. Give them opportunities where they can say, 'I did that!' — instead of seeing
them as kids who need to be kept out of the way because
they keep messing up."

Last May, a public high school in my town provided
such an opportunity for one hundred students. In less than an
hour, under the guidance of an activities director, they painted
a house selected earlier. The local newspaper reported: "A bright
red flatbed truck carried the painters, who held signs reading
'Hand in hand with the community.' The activities director
commented, 'The kids really wanted to do it. . . . This kind
of thing puts the spark back into life.' "[2] Why not a practical,
helpful project like this for church teens?

In missions. "In our culture, young people are turned
inward," says Morris Dirks. "They're encouraged by the culture
that surrounds them to satisfy themselves through a self-centered
pursuit of pleasure." When they can't fully attain that goal, he
says, they can become discouraged and depressed.

"One of the best things we can do for teenagers is to
move them into an environment where they see needs greater
than their own and they begin to lose themselves in the lives
of other people. We took twenty-eight young people to Quito,
Ecuador. They saw the slums of Quito and poverty-stricken
people who live in the mountains. In that setting, it seemed
absurd for young people to talk about being upset because they
didn't have the right kind of clothes. Whatever we can do to
help young people move beyond their sheltered world so they
can get their problems in perspective is important."

This group of teens worked in their denomination's
missionary school — cleaning, painting, sanding — working
on the grounds as well as in churches in the area. "They also
took a trip into the mountains of Ecuador and saw evangelism
in a way they'd never seen it before," Dirks says.

In a dugout canoe, they crossed a river into a village
with thatched huts where they met a missionary who'd been
translating the Bible for some twenty years. "We saw how
Christ had transformed villagers' lives. In that setting, young
people began to get life into perspective. They wanted to get
their sleeping bags and spend time with those Indians even
though they couldn't communicate with them, because they
knew something real was happening."

BRINGING IT HOME

Study 1 Corinthians 12:12-26. What attitudes need to be changed so you'll see teens more clearly as an important part of Christ's Body? Think of two things you can do to expedite this.

Does your church provide times for adults and youth to build relationships? If so, how can you take better advantage of those times? If not, talk with a key person in church about the need for such times.

Ask the youth leader what the main needs of the youth ministry are in the church. What's one way you can help? Drive a car on an outing? Tell the group what it means to be a Christian on your job? Open your home? Be a prayer partner for a teen?

Does your church provide opportunities for teens to participate in the program? How could a teen assist you in a job you do for the church? What about suggesting a brainstorming session to come up with ways the church could integrate teens into its program, not as spectators but as participants? What about community projects? Missionary projects?

12

THE CHURCH'S ROLE IN EDUCATION AND PREVENTION

Even though a desperate teen is adopted by a caring Christian community, that's not enough. Still the youth has to go home. And what if home is a tension-ridden environment peopled by adults who are busy licking their own wounds, or who are trying to raise their children but have never really learned how?

We can't go home with them, but we can help desperate teens by offering to teach their primary care people parenting skills — practical, how-to techniques based soundly on scriptural principles taught by those well-educated in the subject.

Idyllic presentations of the Christian family as a "bit of heaven on earth" with Mama and Daddy and children each fulfilling their responsibilities won't do. Mama may be alcoholic or Daddy emotionally unstable. An aged grandmother may have assumed the role of parent because there was no one else.

Jesus viewed the people He taught realistically and applied the principles of the kingdom of God to their less-than-ideal, real-life circumstances.

PARENTING CLASSES

To wait until teens enter puberty and its peer-dominant society, when doors to their selves begin to shut one by one, is to wait too long. Begin rather by offering parenting classes for those whose children are small. One church I know of has organized a Mother's Club that meets regularly to teach every conceivable phase of parenting young children and provides opportunities for mothers themselves to share what they've learned along the way. Others offer Sunday school electives to both parents where experiences can be shared and practical ways of applying principles worked out and reported.

But it gets harder as children get older. Parents flounder. Christians, especially, suppose: *My children should not be acting like this. I should be able to keep them under control.*

Film series, expert speakers, and discussion groups using well-written guides can be a big help. These can also be effective as outreach ministries to the community.

Those outside the church probably won't come, however, unless someone loves them there. And they'll need someone to come alongside and patiently help them see how to integrate the teachings into their child care.

Educate teens about parents and parents about teens. Help youth understand the stress parents are going through and parents to understand the stress youth experience. Mid-life crisis and puberty. *We are more alike than different. We both are struggling with life changes and aren't sure how to get through.*

What to teach primary care people about parenting adolescents?

- The facts about puberty.
- Basic human needs of adolescents and how to help meet those needs.
- A teenager's emotional makeup.
- How to teach values.
- How to become parents who can demonstrate love in ways the teen needs to see.
- Ways to achieve a balance in setting limits.
- How to help teens make wise choices.
- Skills to help relate to youth as individuals.
- Tips on providing a healthy home life.
- Ways to be friends with teens.

- About teenage rebellion: discriminating between normal and destructive rebellion.
- To reassess parental expectation.
- What to do when behavioral problems erupt.
- To cultivate a young person's potential.
- To differentiate between discipline and punishment.
- How to teach spiritual truths effectively.

UPGRADING EDUCATIONAL PROGRAMS

"Teach pupils, not curriculum." I was young and in charge of the Christian education program in the church. She was one of my teachers. I was disturbed because she wasn't completing the lessons. She was a retired schoolteacher who had learned her profession well and was kindly but firmly helping me understand what teaching was all about.

Her words helped me realize that these were real human beings sitting in the chairs in that Sunday school room. One child may be struggling to survive despite an alcoholic father, another may be secretly snorting cocaine to escape reality, still another may be experimenting with ways to tie a hangman's noose.

She wanted me to remember that Christian educational material cannot be slathered on like ointment to be absorbed through the pores. It must be borne by the Spirit into the human spirit. Not canned lessons. Words on which you've reflected before God so they become *your* words, taught to real human beings who may be tired of trying to make life work one more day. *You are not a body in a seat. You are a person about whom I care. I know you have feelings and a life outside this room that may be less than ideal.*

But being a teacher who believes what you teach, one who loves the students, isn't enough. The following questions may uncover other areas that need attention.

1. Does your church have an up-to-date teacher training program?

Can one be established in the near future? If training is spotty or inadequate, a teacher is responsible to request better training; and if it's not forthcoming, to train himself by attending seminars, taking correspondence courses, reading books on the subject and/or apprenticing with a trained, experienced teacher. Troubled youth do not concentrate well. Teachers need finely-honed skills to get and keep their attention.

2. Are youth learning key concepts and not merely facts about the Bible?

Stuffing facts about the Scriptures into teenage heads may make Sunday school staff feel successful. But success is reaching inside their spirits by the Holy Spirit of God. Some important truths desperate teens need to know are:

● Christ is alive. He is Savior and Lord.

● The Holy Spirit is friend and comforter. For youth who feel alone and afraid, the concept of God as friend can have a powerful impact.

● The Bible is inspired and authoritative. Young people can learn to use it themselves. God Almighty will speak to them through its pages. From it, they can receive help with their problems.

● Every person's life can be fulfilling and purposeful. Particular incidents may be tragic, but even these are under His control.

● Death is separation — a change from one state to another. The human spirit is eternal and will exist in fellowship with God or separated from Him.

● God wants an abiding, intimate relationship with them.

● Prayer is dialogue with God — a way to know His will and enjoy His company.

● Change of character is possible through a Spirit-filled life. So is the ability to experience peace instead of fear. Joy instead of unhappiness.

● Every Christian is gifted and can make a significant contribution to others through ministry.

3. Do your teaching methods communicate?

Are lessons doled out like stale bread? Youth who are shut up inside themselves with anxieties too big to handle need to be drawn out, not preached to. Try dialogue, panels, skits, role play; brainstorm with creative Christians you know for new ways to present old truths. Ask teens themselves. Look for new teaching aids on the market.

Emphasize youth outreach programs. There are suicidal kids within the church, but there are more outside. Has your church developed a plan to reach out to the unchurched in your area?

"A good ministry is constantly checking itself to make sure it isn't falling into the temptation of working only with the Christian kids," Rod Berg says. "When we go to a campus, it is fun just to mill around with the kids who have their spiritual lives together. They're warm and fuzzy and think you're the greatest. It's much more difficult to develop relationships with non-Christians and keep an ongoing ministry with that group."

In a seminar, Rich Van Pelt, founder of Road Home Ministries, commented that teenagers no longer separate in two groups in school — the "in" group and the "out" group. These days, they separate into clusters — the athletic ones, the intellectuals, those who belong to a certain club, etc. To reach each group, he says, churches need to build a balanced youth team so they'll have workers to reach them all — even the punkers.

Are workers available to teens? It was late at night when the phone rang. My husband, then pastor of a northwestern church, answered and heard a weak, desperate voice on the other end. "I was going to let it ring twice. If no one answered, I was going to go home and kill myself. The gun was already loaded," the person said later. He had been extremely depressed and saw no hope for the future.

But because my husband did answer the phone, tragedy was averted. "I'm horrified to find out how often in large churches no one *is* available," one man told me. "Last week, I called a church and asked to speak to the senior pastor and was told he was away. So I asked to speak with the other pastors in turn and was told they were all either in conference or otherwise unavailable. Suppose I had been a desperate teenager looking for help, ready to pull the trigger if I didn't get it?"

It's unfair to expect the pastor or youth leader to be available all the time. But churches can arrange for some adequately trained staff member to be there the way other helping professions do. "I'm meeting with a pastor in that church to talk about setting up such a system," my friend told me.

An effective youth ministry has a high ratio of workers to youth. "We try to keep the ratio of youth workers to teens one to eight" a successful youth pastor told me. "Their primary responsibility is to spot lonely youth and keep them from falling through the cracks."

PREVENTION PROGRAMS

Are people in the church informed about teen suicide? Pastoral staff? Youth workers? Educators? Other adults? Teens themselves? Until now, Christians have largely left the job of education about suicide prevention to secular organizations.

It's time the church became actively involved in suicide prevention again. The following are ideas for prevention programs.

● Suicide prevention training for pastoral staff as well as all church workers. That includes secretaries (who may be the one to take the call from a suicidal teen), educational workers and other volunteer staff members. Be sure every person receives the training. A local counselor, physician or other mental health professional who is well-informed on the subject could conduct the program.

● Sponsor suicide prevention and intervention seminars for the people in the pews. Invite mental health professionals to head them up.

● Make suicide prevention literature available to the congregation. Post lists of suicide prevention organizations and hotlines (see appendix).

● Invite a professional to address parenting classes, men's and women's meetings, leadership meetings, Christian education planning times. Always be sure the subject is presented from a biblical perspective.

● Show a film like *The Question*, available for rental from Youth for Christ. This film portrays the reaction of Will, a high school senior, to the suicide of his college-age brother.

● Give the subject priority on the agenda of denominational and interchurch conventions. Appoint a committee to research the issue and come up with recommendations.

● Provide networking sessions. Use the parable of the Good Samaritan and its modern counterpart in chapter 10 as a springboard for discussion. Show how networking operates. Use the illustration of a hospital staff and apply it to a teenager's world.

Make these "learn-and-do" sessions in which members actually begin to establish friendships with teenagers: with

extended family, with neighbors, with those in the church.
Have members report back to the group.

• Provide troubled teens and their parents or guardians
with access to names of trained, professional counselors. Some
large churches have a counselor on staff or invite one to locate
on church premises. Other churches should have available a
list of qualified professionals whom they can recommend.

Some pastors are qualified to act as interventionists,
while others are not. Neither a pastor nor anyone else should
hesitate to call in a psychologist or psychiatrist when it's
necessary. *A teen's life may be at stake.* The therapist should
be well-recommended, preferably a Christian. A Christian counselor will have a biblical world view and advise according to
biblical principles.

One parent whose teenager committed suicide told me
emphatically that one thing she'd do differently would be to
choose the counselor to whom she sent her child much more
carefully.

• Train lay counselors in the congregation. The program
Bill Davis and his associates have taught includes basic counseling skills such as active listening, clarification and confron-
tation. It also includes teaching about different kinds of problems
such as alcoholism and suicide. He emphasizes the fact that
lay counselors need to be sensitive to their limitations.

Such lay counseling programs may be available at local
Bible schools, presented in conjunction with a church by a
professional counselor or as a course offered at a local counseling
center. Davis believes that much can be done to help troubled
youth within the church if individuals have a minimum amount
of training and know what to look for and how to respond.

• Make adequate counseling available to every teen
who needs it and for their parents or guardians, too, if necessary.
Consider establishing a scholarship fund for such families.
What local mental health services are available to those with
limited incomes? What state agencies and facilities? Counseling
centers?

• Discuss the possibility of establishing a local hotline
sponsored, perhaps, by the area ministerial association in conjunction with other parachurch organizations. CONTACT Tele-
ministries, USA, Inc., is a Christian-based, 24-hour telephone
help line organization with approximately ninety offices nation-

wide. Volunteers who have been carefully trained and are accredited man the phones to listen and counsel.

New chapters can be started by a local ministerial association, council of churches, large church or group of churches working cooperatively. CONTACT'S national office can provide guidelines in getting started and instructing you in the process. Every center must be locally supported. A modest fee is charged to become a CONTACT center, plus a small annual fee; and local leaders must sign the organization's covenant.

Some local CONTACT organizations advertise themselves as Christian ministries. Others, while supported by local churches, do not. Volunteers do not preach over the phone, but are to be willing to help with spiritual matters if a caller requests it. For more information about starting a CONTACT center or to locate the nearest hotline, write CONTACT Tele-ministries USA, Inc., Pouch A., Harrisburg, PA 17105.

Another organization that offers guidelines is The American Association of Suicidology. Write: The American Association of Suicidology, 2459 S. Ash, Denver, CO 80222.

● Can churches in your area open a walk-in center? One of the most well-known is operated by the Samaritans (not a religious organization). Program coordinator Ellen Zold says:

"Our daily walk-in service is available from 8 A.M. to 8 P.M. Anyone who would like to is invited to come in or call our center to take advantage of the opportunity to talk with a carefully selected, trained volunteer. An appointment is not necessary. It is not a substitute for counseling or psychotherapy, but rather an opportunity to talk with someone in person or over the telephone and receive support for whatever difficulties an individual is currently experiencing. There is no limit to the amount of visits or calls a person may come in for."[2]

● Organize a self-help group for parents of depressed teens. The pastor who organized one such group began with two families who had troubled youth. They began to meet once a week and eventually other parents joined them. Recently, one of the members said, "I couldn't have made it this year had it not been for the group." The pressure was so great she wasn't sure her marriage would have survived otherwise. The pastor commented, "They don't just stroke each other but are very committed to helping each other deal with the problem."

● Provide information about self-help groups in the community for teens with drinking and drug problems. Be sensitive to the fact that substance abuse may mean that an adolescent is depressed and needs help in dealing with his emotions and the causes for his depression.

● Be aware that there may be depressed — even suicidal — youth in your own congregation. Establish a networking system so that Sunday school teachers and others who suspect a teen has a problem will know what to do.

● Provide peer counseling training for key, mature young people. They are the ones a depressed youth is most likely to confide in when thinking of suicide.

"At my school, they have what we call 'natural helpers,' one teen said. "They're students who are there to listen and help."

● If your church does not have a prayer chain, institute one. *Make sure every member keeps prayer requests private, however.* Pastors, youth leaders, Sunday school teachers and others should all be praying for these adolescents. Pray also as your church institutes a training program, that God will be in charge and that common sense, not alarmism, will prevail.

Some professionals have reservations about current suicide prevention programs. Others feel that publicity is detrimental. They worry that publicity or wrongly conducted programs might have a negative influence on the more fragile youth and encourage them to act on suicidal impulses. At this writing, a large scale evaluation has not been done.

ASSURING POSITIVE EFFECTS

● In discussions of suicide, avoid sensationalizing the subject. Avoid romanticizing those who have taken their own lives or made attempts. Vulnerable youth must not be encouraged to believe that suicide is a way to get the attention they've been looking for but never found. If violent actions are all they know and these actions do receive the spotlight, they may repeat them. Help provide alternatives to self-destruction as a solution to their pain.

● Some groups may wish to teach a "How to Cope With Stress" program to their youth that teaches the symptoms of depression and provides opportunities for the youth to receive help. Mature teens are selected from the group for education in suicide intervention.

● Include postvention programs when a suicide has taken place in school or church so that young people can talk it out with a trained adult. Emphasize the terrible destructiveness of such action to avoid a "trigger" effect. Provide positive solutions for depressed adolescents and opportunities for them to talk with someone who can help following such a session.

● Use only people trained in suicidology to head up prevention programs. Take the latest research in the field into consideration when making plans.

● Evaluate suicide prevention programs regularly to determine their effectiveness and changes and improvements that should be made.

BRINGING IT HOME

What opportunities are available in your church or community for parents to learn biblically-based child rearing skills? Is there a need for such a class or small self-help group? Ask the proper staff person for ideas.

Review the important truths teens need to know. Choose ones *you* need to integrate into your life and look up key words in your concordance. Ask God to help you apply them to your life *now.* Share in a personal testimony in church a way your attitude in one of these areas has changed.

Has your church discussed teen suicide prevention and intervention? What needs to be done? Share ideas from the list with the proper church staff person and ask how you can help expedite one of them. If no education program has been instituted, start with basics, such as obtaining brochures from suicide prevention organizations or putting together a list of helps available in your area.

13

SUICIDE AND SCRIPTURE

Imagine yourself in the following scene:

You are leading a group of teens and one says he can't see any reason why people don't have a right to commit suicide if they choose. "It's my life, isn't it?" What will you answer? What would you tell a youth who says life will be better in heaven and it's awful for him down here so it's OK to hurry things along so he can be with God?

A friend of mine had to figure it out fast. "A teenage girl who was staying with my family was pretty depressed. She simply couldn't understand why it wasn't OK for her to take her own life. She was a professing Christian, and so far as she could see, she would be bettering herself. Instead of fighting through all the troubles that seemed to be plaguing her, she'd be with the Lord where things would be perfect. Wasn't that her destination anyway? What made it worse was that a close friend had committed suicide some time before. Following her friend's example seemed like a logical option to her."

Fortunately, my friend and her husband had answers. "But working with her was *hard*," she recalls. After all, there *is* no verse in Scripture that states plainly, "Thou shalt not commit suicide."

LIFE FROM GOD

This couple could count on plenty of Scriptures, though, which affirm that life is a gift from God.

"The Lord God formed man from the dust of the ground and breathed into his nostrils the breath of life, and man became a living being" (Genesis 2:7).

"Through him all things were made; without him nothing was made that has been made" (John 1:3). Life is a precious gift to be cherished.

The one who gives life is the only one with authority to take it. "The Lord brings death and makes alive; he brings down to the grave and raises up" (1 Samuel 2:6).

"When you send your spirit, they are created and you renew the face of the earth" (Psalm 104:30).

It may seem pretty obvious to us adults who've grown up as Christians that life comes from God and belongs to Him, not us. But it may not be something youth "just know."

Don't expect them to shed their existential mindset that life is valueless and come running open-armed to embrace the idea. Why should they when they've grown up in a world where mankind has been marked down and tossed on the bargain counter?

SUICIDE IS NOT A CHOICE

Debbie Boone says, "I'm not so far from adolescence that I don't remember times of deep pain, sitting in dark corners wondering if there was any hope for my life.

"If I were still in high school or junior high school and I saw young people taking their lives, I would begin to wonder in my down moments — is life worth living? Did they do the right thing?"[1]

Melissa's counselor had to convince her teenage client that to kill herself would be wrong. By age seventeen, Melissa had made two suicide attempts. Illegitimate and born when her mother was fifteen, Melissa became the victim of that parent's angry outbursts during a tumultuous early life.

Then, when her mother married and gave birth to a

boy, Melissa became jealous of the attention he received. It was after her second suicide attempt that Juanita, the counselor (and a Christian), helped Melissa work through her feelings of rejection.

Juanita explained that both Melissa and her mother were blaming each other for making life miserable. "Satan had dominion over our lives. We were being mastered by sin. My drinking and getting high was sin. Even my attempts at suicide were sin."

Melissa invited Christ into her life. "Two months after my release from the hospital [where the counselor worked with her] my mother, her husband and my brother all asked Jesus to forgive them of their sins . . . My story has a happy ending."[2]

So there will be more happy endings, teens need to know that suicide is not an option. The sixth commandment, "Thou shalt not kill" is more accurately translated "You shall not murder." And that "the criminality of the act consists in its being an assault upon the image of God (Genesis 9:6) . . . The prohibition includes not only killing of a fellowman, but the destruction of one's own life, or suicide."[3] That makes suicide not a moral choice, but self-murder.

Men in the Bible did commit suicide and God didn't speak out against it. Saul ordered his armor-bearer to kill him so the king wouldn't be taken prisoner. Ahithophel put his house in order and hanged himself. Zimri set the palace afire and went up in flames with it. Judas hanged himself.

But that's the way history is written — inspired and uninspired alike. Incidents like incest and murder are recorded the same way in Scripture. God expects the reader to evaluate his own morality or immorality by applying the standards He sets elsewhere in the Bible.

WHEN LIFE HURTS

Troubled youth need to see that, even when life hurts, God's followers in Scripture never even alluded to suicide as an out. Job lost family, wealth and health and cursed the day he was born, but never did he take steps to end his life. Instead, he declared, "Man's days are determined: you have decreed the number of months" (Job 14:5).

The same is true for the apostle Paul. Five times he received thirty-nine lashes. Three times he was beaten with rods. Once he was stoned. Three times he was shipwrecked. He went hungry, cold and naked. He was imprisoned. Nothing he wrote endorses suicide.

That was true even when he was an old man, in prison, tired and weak as a result of continual persecution, knowing that death was imminent. "For I am already being poured out like a drink offering, and the time has come for my departure. I have fought the good fight, I have finished the race, I have kept the faith" (2 Timothy 4:6,7). What counted to him was not to drop out of the race but to complete it. Handling the hurts of life, he intimated, isn't always easy, but it is worth it.

Another reason suicide is out of the question is that "Your body is a temple of the Holy Spirit, who is in you, whom you have received from God . . . You are not your own; you were bought at a price. Therefore, honor God with your body"(1 Corinthians 6:19,20).

Rather than destroy their bodies, Christians are urged to offer their bodies as living sacrifices (Romans 12:1). In his last days, Paul practiced what he preached. He knew he'd probably be murdered by the Romans. From his earlier experiences, he knew the kind of terrible pain that would mean. But his body was not his own. It belonged to God. So he'd minister as long as God gave him life, no matter what the circumstances. And wait for heaven until it was God's time for him to go there.

Heaven is certainly worth waiting for. And that's the emphasis in Christ's preaching: *Watch, wait and work until I come.* Anticipate the future and be occupied with humanity's needs in the present.

BRINGING IT HOME

What *would* you tell a teen who says, "It's my life, isn't it? Why can't I end it and go to a better place?"

● Only God has the right to take life. It's a gift from Him, not an accident.

● Suicide is self-murder.

● Every individual is accountable to God for what they did with their life.

● God recounts times in the Bible when people committed suicide, but He never condones it.

● Godly biblical characters accepted suffering as part of life. Their goal was to trust and love God even when life hurts. Their lives show us that we can make it through anything if we live close to Him and let Him help us.

 • God doesn't talk about the wrongness of suicide in the Bible because He emphasizes its opposite: life. Study the following verses about life. What kind of statement do they make against suicide?

"Therefore I tell you, do not worry about your life , what you will eat or drink; or about your body, what you will wear. Is not life more important than food, and the body more important than clothes? Look at the birds of the air; they do not sow or reap or store away in barns, and yet your heavenly Father feeds them. Are you not much more valuable then they?" (Matthew 6:25,26).

"And even the very hairs of your head are all numbered. So don't be afraid; you are worth more than many sparrows" (Matthew 10:30,31).

"I have come that they may have life, and have it to the full" (John 10:10).

14

HOW GOVERNMENT
AND SCHOOLS CAN HELP

I grew up in the "God Bless America" era when national holidays meant parades and waving flags. A minute of silence on Memorial Day. Wreaths placed on the graves of the war dead by friends in the American Legion while the rest of us townspeople looked on. Community-wide picnics on July 4.

Because of Vietnam, Watergate and their kin, for my sons and their contemporaries, national pride deteriorated to national disenchantment. They do not know the feeling of identity in America that I experienced as a young girl as I let the huge flag Grandpa displayed on his front porch blow around me.

NATIONAL ROOTS

But that "long national nightmare" of the late 60's and early 70's has given way to a renewed sense of patriotism. And the church can take the lead in encouraging love of country again. A once-a-year splash of red, white and blue isn't enough. What our youth need is genuine love of country from hearts that are convinced. Why not sing the patriotic hymns at the

back of the hymnal? Celebrate important holidays? Be un-
ashamedly patriotic? Call for prayer for our nation and its
leaders? Give our sons and daughters back their sense of place
and continuity, love of homeland?

VIRTUE

While the freedom of religion is an important democratic
principle, that does not preclude the teaching of virtue by
secular institutions. Moral excellence. Goodness of character —
especially honesty, industriousness and purity.

These are characteristics that came over on the May-
flower and were held up by our founders as vital to the well-
being of individuals and the nation they formed. Not that our
American fathers were all scrupulously pure or without warped
ways. But they mostly knew what was moral and what was
not. The word was not a vague, subjective term no man could
define for the group.

That concept of virtue has been distorted and exploited
until it seems out of place and outdated. Now, as a consequence,
no man dares define obscenity for the nation, because "you
can't legislate morality." Good and evil have melded and produced an amoral society into which we've birthed our children.

But the right to set the tone of America's moral climate
is still in the hands of the people.

NATIONAL GOVERNMENT

The right to ask for the government to take preventive
action against teenage suicide belongs to the people, too. At
this writing, Congress is considering a proposal from the Public
Health Services that would develop and publish information
about the causes of suicide of those under twenty-one years,
and ways of preventing it. That information would be made
available to the public and to health professionals along with
an evaluation of suicide prevention activities.

As citizens, we need to keep in touch with the disposition of such proposals. *Are* the needs of youth being kept
before legislators? Is appropriate action being taken?

STATE GOVERNMENT

The first two states to pass legislation requiring schools

to offer suicide prevention programs on a secondary level are Florida and California. Florida classes are offered to freshman and sophomore students. Instructors must be certified in suicide prevention.

California's bill provides for the development of a statewide youth suicide prevention program with two demonstration programs, one in San Mateo and one in Los Angeles.

New York State's Youth Suicide Prevention Council published their Interim Report in 1985 and made recommendations that the state do the following:

● Bring together evaluation strategy and prevention programs.

● Develop a clearinghouse of prevention information.

● Consider supporting research of critical topics regarding teen suicide prevention.

● Include an evaluation component in New York State's funded program.

● Educate media groups regarding their role in preventing teenage suicide.

● Conduct or support a study of the reporting and surveillance of teenage suicide attempts and completions as well as hospital emergency room practices.

● Conduct or support a study of the regulations governing the reporting and confidentiality of reports by medical examiners of possible suicide deaths.

EDUCATION

Another area of importance is the educational system our nation provides its youth. It has a powerful impact on the forming of their attitudes toward life. Seminary faculty member Ronald B. Allen reminds us how far we have fallen when he writes, "Education in the early colonies was oriented toward the glory of God."[1]

Today's secular school system has been largely washed and spun dry of any idea that a Greater Other — one from whom life is a gift — even exists.

Evolution is taught as fact, not theory. In many schools this means, for one thing, that creationism has little chance of being taught as an alternative to evolution. This compounded the problems of one already depressed, withdrawn girl who was raised in a Christian home and taught that God was the originator of life. She didn't reveal her confusion until she began getting well and poured over books written by Christians that refuted evolution on reasonable grounds and showed the strong cause for creationism.

Prayer and Bible study are no longer allowed. It means also that there is no prayer in schools. God is not mentioned in the context of faith. Bible and prayer groups are losing the battle to meet on school campuses. Now, in my city, the practice of holding baccalaureate services at graduation may be phased out.

As a result, the message sent to our youth at the ringing of the school bell is a humanistic one, a secular world view. *Man is in the center of the universe.* You are to make your own destiny. Success, in a world too chaotic for adults to handle, is up to you.

THINGS TO DO

Teachers and parents. An estimated 500,000 Christian teachers work in the public education system. Although local restrictions vary, they can still do much to present the Christian perspective. Kim Colby of the Christian Legal Society says, "A school may sponsor the *study* of religion, but not the *practice* of religion. . . . The school may *expose* students to all religious views, but may not *impose* any particular views."[2] The group also states that a teacher "may discuss his or her personal beliefs *when they are relevant* to the subject matter." But that must be done with wisdom and care.[3]

Use of the Bible. Israel is an example of one country where the Bible is taught from kindergarten through twelfth grade (and Israel has a lower rate of suicide). It is presented in Hebrew classes, Talmud, history, literature, and others. But in the United States, since classroom emphasis on any of the three major world theisms as a values system has been removed, suicide has trebled.

Creationism as a viable alternative to evolution. The battle to have evolution presented only as a theory and creationism given equal time has been fought fiercely since the "Monkey Trials." Where do the public schools in your area stand?

Parent participation in school life. What curriculum is being used in various classes? Is "values clarification" being taught? How? What is the classroom philosophy of teachers? The tone of sex education? Is birth control information being disseminated? Birth control devices being distributed? What about prayer in schools? Baccalaureate services? Drug use and sale? Are basic virtues being taught? Bible clubs or prayer groups allowed to meet on campus?

SCHOOL COUNSELORS

School counselors may be the first professionals to talk to a depressed teen. Robert J. McBrien, director of counseling services at Salisbury State College, says that they "are perhaps the only school professionals with training in suicide prevention."[4] They should, therefore, be informed when a youth has experienced a life crisis. But one parent of a self-destructive youth complained that the counselor in her school seemed unsure how to handle the situation, and didn't seem to have enough time.

Here's what one group of teens told me:

"School guidance counselors are too busy to help with problems. They just help with grades. They don't have much time to listen, and they can't help everyone. I think they need more staff. Kids don't go to them because they know they don't have time."

How about the program in your area? Is there an adequate number of well-trained, compassionate counselors on staff? What philosophies influence the counsel they give?

SCHOOL NURSE

A school nurse could also be the person who spots a depressed student. Do the ones in your school have the time and skills in adolescent behavior and in communication to play their role effectively? Is there good communication between nurse and family members?

A professional nursing journal on teen suicide asserts, "The nurse must encourage the development of a network of supportive family members, friends and health care professionals who will be consistent in their approach. The nurse must foster the notion that all members of a network are responsible."[5]

A UNIQUE SCHOOL PROGRAM

Victor M. Victoroff is one medical professional who is going into schools to do something about youth suicide. A psychiatrist who is chief of the psychiatric division of the Huron Road Hospital, he began to give his now well-known seminars at high schools and colleges twelve years ago. Since then he has addressed almost four thousand students.

"Students are admonished 'not to kill each other.' They are reminded that simple-minded sadistic teasing of certain members of their school population can traumatize vulnerable avoidant youngsters to the point that their loneliness and isolation can lead to suicide."[6]

But Dr. Victoroff doesn't rely only on words. He shows some of the emergency room equipment that is used on suicidal patients — like tracheotomy kits, stomach pumps, suture kits, spinal needles, suction machines, emesis basins.

Then the most publicized portion of his program begins: a visual presentation of autopsy material. (Students who wish to leave may do so at this time.) The color pictures Dr. Victoroff has chosen to flash on the screen are graphic and shocking: victims who have died from strangulation, knifing, poisoning, electrocution, asphyxiation and gunshot wounds. His purpose is clearly to confront students with a realistic view of suicide instead of an unrealistic, romanticized one. "The lecture concludes with a plea to respect life, one's own and another's, and for each member of the audience to become a basic rescuer of suicidal persons in their experience."[7]

At a seminar at Huron Road Hospital in October, 1980 titled "Suicide in Adolescents" in which Dr. Victoroff participated, the following recommendations were made:

● Establish a program. Expand crisis intervention. Increase public awareness. Identify the suicide-prone in the school community. Trained mental health professionals should be engaged by the schools. Sponsor creative social research.

● Report and identify the problem on bulletin boards, in school papers, class discussion and assignments.

● Make parents aware.

● When an attempted suicide occurs, it should be openly discussed and its effects exposed.

● Vulnerable students should be identified and coded.

● Encourage use of the 'school grapevine' — an informal route by which rumors can be identified, published and traced.

● A particular person should be appointed at each school whose name would be published as a receiver of confidential information. He or she would act as receiver of news that a person is suicidal and have sufficient training to know what to do with this information.

● Members of the student body might be chosen to act as student ombudsmen who might be an important link between students who don't want to talk to adults but need help, and the authority where rescue could be obtained.[8]

OTHER SCHOOL PROGRAMS

The Fairfax County, Virginia, Adolescent Suicide Prevention Program was founded after eleven teens in the area committed suicide in the 1981-1982 school year and another eight deaths were recorded during the summer.

A 400-square-mile, mostly middle-class community, it has the tenth largest local school district in the nation, with 124,000 students in 162 schools. A suicide prevention coordinator was appointed in each school and training workshops held for them and all who counseled students. Teacher training sessions were conducted. Parent training programs sponsored by community groups were offered. Teen awareness programs were instituted. So was a student stress program, presented by students but planned in conjunction with professionals.

After the first year, the program was evaluated and in 1983, the scope of the suicide prevention program extended to include seventh and eighth grades as well.

Plano, Texas, has introduced several programs into its schools. In 1982, under school leadership, students formed SWAT (Students Working All Together), a student-helping-student program. SWAT team members receive phone numbers of new students, welcome them to the community and invite them to Newcomers Club where they receive a coupon book that includes tickets for a free school lunch, free admission to a school activity, etc. In a variety of ways, they build relationships that help alleviate the stress of getting accustomed to a new school.

SWAT instituted BIONIC, a button and poster campaign. Posters and buttons both bear the acronym that stands for "Believe It or Not, I Care." BIONIC members send get-well cards to students and teachers, helped start a Students Against Drunk Driving group and help others uncover reasons for unacceptable behavior.

Because of the success of SWAT, a parent's group was formed to welcome new families to the school district and establish links between parents and provide an awareness of student needs.

The A TEAM is another student group ("A" stands for "academic") — this one for students with special academic skills. Coaches encourage excellence and help students realize their potential.

Bergen County, New Jersey, introduced its own suicide prevention program, titled ASAP (Adolescent Suicide Awareness Program). Introduced in 1980, the program provides suicide prevention training by health care professionals for educators, parents and some students. The program also expedites professional counseling for students who need it. In schools where a suicide occurs, it helps students deal with the aftershock.

Diane Ryerson, the program's director, says, "We measure our success by the number of kids who come up to us after a seminar or classroom discussion and say they have a friend who might be suicidal, and by the kids who come up themselves and say they have been feeling depressed and want help dealing with their feelings."[9]

The goal for such programs is to network with parents and others in order to help avert tragedies like the two that follow.

Ron and Kevin were students in the same western high school. Ron was outgoing and excelled in sports; Kevin was quieter, a listener, and active in the school's music program. Both boys were outstanding students; both were compassionate toward others.

Kevin's life was thrown into turmoil when his parents were divorced. Things became worse for him when his mother opposed his dating a girl he said he cared deeply about.

"If Ron experienced any losses, I don't know what they are," the teacher who told me about the boys said.

All the reasons will probably never be known. But Ron and Kevin — gifted students with life ahead of them — both committed suicide. Kevin shot himself on the way to school. Ron took an overdose of pills.

CHRISTIAN SCHOOLS

One institution with the potential to make a significant impact is the Christian school.

"The most important thing is the atmosphere of the school itself," one teacher in a Christian school told me. "I've seen students get terribly depressed because a Christian school was so rule-oriented as to how to dress and what to say."

The school in which she teaches is not like that. From time to time, she did spot students who seemed depressed — "observers on the scene" rather than participants. "I'd talk with them, communicate that they weren't getting involved and ask if there was anything I could do. When appropriate, I talked with their parents. And I kept on loving them."

Bob Bowers, former principal of Salem Academy, a Christian school in Salem, Oregon, says that one of its strengths is that all the teacher models are Christians. "And most of the students have strong Christian commitments. Sometimes when a depressed student comes along, the others are there to encourage him or her.

"When a faculty member does get word about a troubled student, faculty make it a matter of prayer immediately. Those who are close to that student will get next to him."

The difference in curriculum with public schools? "Whenever there's a concept, whether in math, science or history, that can be illustrated by biblical principles, it will be integrated into the regular subject matter. Constants, for example — things you can always rely on. Those are set by God. Social studies and ethics are subjects into which it would be easy to integrate scriptural principles. Bible is taught as a separate subject as well."

The principal of one California Christian school says his staff is monitoring suicide prevention programs in public schools. His school plans to put together its own program using a biblical approach, emphasizing the key role parents play as authorities, and then training selected, mature students.

BRINGING IT HOME

Has your state passed legislation to institute suicide prevention programs? Write your legislator to find out what's being done.

Visit a local high school. Eat lunch in the cafeteria. Find out answers to some of the questions in this chapter.

Talk with a Christian teacher and find out how you can pray for him.

Have schools in your area instituted stress management instruction or suicide prevention programs? If a teen has committed suicide in the area, has there been postvention instruction for students to reduce possible cluster suicides? Contact the local parent-teacher's association and school board members for more information.

15

WHEN · AN EMERGENCY STRIKES

Vivienne Loomis was fourteen years old when she hanged herself.

The idea of death didn't come to her suddenly. On November 9, 1971, when she learned that her favorite teacher and confidante, John May, would be leaving, she wrote, "It seems like I ought to die now while the going's good."[1]

She made several attempts. Once, she swallowed pills. In a diary entry dated December 11, 1973, she described attempts at self-strangulation.

"DEATH IS GOING TO BE A BEAUTIFUL THING," she wrote across the bathroom wall after one attempt to strangle herself. During the half hour spent in the bathroom on that occasion, she wrote that she also had been "sending a prayer. The prayer was not strong enough. I never could pray. You can tell when a prayer doesn't get through."[2]

Then, on December 21, 1973, Vivienne Loomis hanged herself.

The daughter of a Unitarian minister and an artistic mother who worked as a metalsmith, Vivienne expressed her feelings of depression and alienation in a diary and in poetry

141

that revealed an unusual giftedness of expression.

John May, with whom she corresponded, tried to make her feel like a valuable person. In her letters, she told him how depressed she felt and about her thoughts of death. He was the one she wrote and told that she'd attempted suicide on December 7, 1973. However, by the time he received the letter, Vivienne was dead.

She also confided her suicidal thoughts to a girlfriend, but the friend felt that she couldn't tell anyone — that it would be betrayal. Vivienne also told her sister but swore her to secrecy as well.

The writers who recount Vivienne's story conclude:

"What if John [her former teacher] had called Vivienne from California and told her that he could not keep her dangerous secret? What if he had phoned Paulette [Vivienne's mother] and warned her to ignore Vivienne's injunction against reading her journal? Could we revise the awful outcome? But life is not like the movies. The reel can't be run again."[3]

Life is *not* like the movies. Neither is it a play we can rehearse until we get it right. There's no opportunity to go back and rewrite a scene after we realize the dialogue wasn't good, or maybe the action. It's one time through.

"If a teen is seriously depressed," says counselor Bill Davis, "what needs to happen needs to happen quickly. You don't have a whole lot of time to bone up."

That's why it's urgent when a teen is suicidal that we get it right the first time.

Remember, teenage is a time when many youth do experience mood swings, feel down temporarily, have trouble making decisions, are emotionally volatile, feel alienated — especially from parents — and spend more time in their own world. But when a teen is in trouble, those symptoms intensify, and other warning signs may be evident as well. The majority of people who kill themselves do give warnings that something is wrong. Those warnings include:

A CHANGE OF BEHAVIOR

In eating habits. Sleeping habits. Socialization. Personality characteristics. A quiet guy, Ken becomes loud and obnoxious. Doretta, usually outgoing, becomes morose.

Margie picks at her food instead of eating heartily the

way she usually does. Or she may show signs of anorexia or bulimia. Maybe she stays up late, watching TV, then you hear her moving restlessly in her room.

Such a teen may act recklessly, driving the car too fast and having narrow scrapes. "I look back and realize he was taking chances the way he rode his bike. I didn't see it then, however," the parent of a teen who committed suicide told me.

Impulsive anyway, a youth may act more impulsively now. Perhaps he quits his job on the spot because of an argument with a co-worker. The worse the pressure on him gets, the more likely he may be to act impulsively.

SIGNS OF DEPRESSION

Lethargy. Sadness. Lack of energy. Withdrawal. Disinterest in things they normally care about. Since depression in teens is often masked, other symptoms may be evident — like disobedience and aberrant behavior. Disobeying curfew. Defying rules. Restlessness, nervousness, inability to concentrate, irritability, fear, anxiety, evidence of guilt feelings and anger, headaches or other physical problems.

MOOD SWINGS

They've had ups and downs since they entered adolescence. But these are more severe and longer-lasting.

PROBLEMS AT SCHOOL

Defying teachers. Skipping school. Going off campus when it's not allowed. Falling grades. Complaints by teachers that work isn't getting done.

USE OF DRUGS AND/OR ALCOHOL

The American Association of Suicidology reports that, "In the Peck and Litman study of adolescent suicides, it was learned that nearly half of the suicidal youngsters were involved in some form of drug or alcohol abuse shortly before their suicidal death. This does not necessarily imply that it was the substance abused that led to the death. Rather, the same factors that made them unhappy enough to commit suicide probably contributed to their abuse of drugs."[4]

Suppose Eva's parents leave her to fend for herself because their business is failing. Lonely and afraid, she turns to food and gains a lot of weight. Kids at school begin to make fun of her. She begins to drink beer and smoke pot in her room at night as an escape. Hating herself and feeling rejected and isolated, she could be a prime candidate for suicide.

PROBLEMS IN COMMUNICATION

A teen becomes silent, refuses to talk about what's on his mind, won't enter into conversations the way he used to. He may become defiant when you do try to talk with him, displaying a "mind your own business" attitude. Or, already quiet, he becomes more so.

SELF-ASSAULTIVE OR SELF-DESTRUCTIVE BEHAVIOR

One counselor told me that he has noted tiny cut marks on the forearms of youth who've come to him for help. They were self-inflicted wounds made with a sharp object. When asked about them, the teens explained that they hurt so bad inside that to cut themselves externally provided a measure of relief.

SUICIDE ATTEMPTS

Statistics vary, but a large percentage of those who commit suicide have made previous attempts. Even though they may have seemed like feeble, attention-getting actions, they are not to be dismissed lightly. Vivienne Loomis experimented repeatedly with suicide before she finally hanged herself. Certainly, this is one of the most reliable signs of risk.

SUICIDE THREATS

"I'm tired of the hassle. Why keep on? I don't have to, either. I have a way to get out of all this." Or a simple statement like, "This family would be better off if I weren't around." The idea that those who threaten suicide don't really mean it is a fallacious one.

GIVING ITEMS AWAY

While the majority of youth do not leave a suicide note, they may do their version of "getting things in order." One way might be to give away a favorite collection of *Mad* magazines, of records or posters.

A youth who has been feeling depressed and hopeless about life for a variety of reasons and then experiences a new loss or undergoes some traumatic experience can suppose death is the only answer. This has been called "the precipitating factor." It could be the death of someone close, or loss of a parent through divorce. It could be the loss of status among peers. Some further indication that they don't belong, that others are completely unaware of their misery, that there's no help for them.

Suppose fifteen-year-old Pam throws her book on the table. "If I don't pass this test, I'll kill myself. I have to get a passing grade to pull down a C." You might dismiss this as just talk, except that you know Pam is a perfectionist. She's been worrying about everything lately and hasn't slept well in weeks. She seems agitated and can't settle down to do the things she used to enjoy. And she's been preoccupied with talk of death. You admit to yourself that Pam is troubled and that this may be more than the ordinary "teenage blues" because you realize that she's showing a combination of signs that something is wrong. Her attitude has been a growing one that seems to have become more acute just recently.

HELP THEM TALK

You shouldn't try to do the job of a trained counselor unless you are one. But you can draw out a youth you suspect might be contemplating suicide by asking questions, particularly about their feelings, that show you are concerned and want to help. You might say, "You seem to be feeling badly and I'm worried. I know things haven't been easy for you lately. How have you been feeling?"

He may be reluctant to talk, but don't give up. My years working with adults in seminars and retreats have shown me how hard it is for those who are depressed to talk about their feelings. ("I was afraid if you knew, you wouldn't accept me," they tell me later.) How much harder it is for adolescents!

So although he does want help, he may refuse to admit

it and even push you away. Be gently persistent. Don't make things worse. Pray and let God guide. And let the person know, by your attitude, expression and action that you won't be judgmental, no matter what they confide. The American Association of Suicidology suggests that you keep leading the conversation with more statements and questions. Try to read his body language, too.

Your job is to build a relationship with the troubled teen that lets him know he can trust you, that you are empathetic and on his side. The American Psychiatric Association points out that suicidal people usually don't want to talk about their feelings and because some people pass suicide off lightly, even joke about it, that makes it harder to admit they're considering it.

Maybe it's hard for you to talk about suicide at all. But to help a youth in trouble, you must get past your uneasiness or call in someone who can talk about it.

One family I know never built communication skills — certainly not about what they really thought and felt. Our children may never have learned to communicate with us because we never learned to communicate either. But if you know they need to talk to someone and they won't talk to you, humble yourself. Invite over the persons with whom they do open up. Make it plain that you need their help and tell them why. Consult a counselor or pastor for advice if needed.

Be honest in conversation with the despairing. One of the easiest ways to relate to them is to tell them, "I was extremely depressed myself," if that's true, without going into details of your experience (it's their problem, not your past woes, they need to center on).

When a youth intimates he is thinking of suicide, it is no time for teens or adults to keep confidences. The troubled person may say, "If you tell, I'll never forgive you." Teens may feel obligated to keep silent; adults may have qualms, too. But countless case histories show that suicidal teens did warn someone who felt they couldn't tell. Other youth gave warnings through their poetry and compositions they wrote for school. But sometimes, teachers only corrected the work and handed it back.

If they do begin to open up, encourage them to tell you more without trying to "set them straight." No preaching that taking one's life is unscriptural. That's true, and they do need to know that, but not now when their feelings are running so high they can't see past them. You want them to tell you what they're thinking and feeling so you can determine what to do next.

Count on God to be present during the conversation, to give strength and wisdom. He cares about teen lives more than you do and wants them to become whole, productive persons. Pray silently before you begin talking, pray with little looks to God while you're talking to the young person, and maintain a prayerful attitude as you listen.

It's important to take the initiative and be confrontive. Talking about suicide — putting it in concrete terms — helps to yank off the romantic notion with which a youth may be clothing it in his mind, and helps him see the incongruity of using it to get revenge or attention.

Direct questions about suicide can be a relief if the individual has been contemplating it so much that the idea has become deeply rooted in his mind. To finally have it brought out in the open, and talked about non-judgmentally, helps rather than hinders.

CRISIS INTERVENTION

Always take every indication seriously that an individual is thinking about suicide. One youth worker told me that early in his career a teen who was having a lot of trouble came to his house and said he was going to take his car on the freeway and kill himself.

"I took his keys away from him. 'You don't have the guts to kill yourself,' I told him.

"The next day, I told someone what had happened. They confronted me. 'How would you feel if he had left you a note that said, "I had the guts" and gone out and rammed his car into a post?' "

The teen did not commit suicide. "But that taught me a lesson I've never forgotten. I've never again taken the words 'I'm going to kill myself' lightly. Even when I feel it's just an empty statement, I take it very seriously."

The more concrete their plans, the more dangerous the situation and the more the need for immediate action. Do they have a weapon stashed somewhere? Have they experimented with fashioning a noose? Even if their plans aren't concrete, youth are notoriously impulsive. They could still grab a gun and pull the trigger and be just as dead.

Suppose you are the one who walks into a crisis situation the way Ed Davies did in the first chapter. *Remove the weapon in a way that doesn't endanger you.* Do not leave the person alone. Stay with the individual or have another responsible person do so while you call for help.

Call on God to help you stay calm. It's not easy dealing with a situation that's potentially life-threatening. If you are thrown into a panic, your anxiety will only inflame the situation.

Take charge. Insist that you're not going to leave the individual, that you will get help and that there's a better answer to his problem than this. Be loving but be firm. Keep talking quietly to maintain contact with him.

When a young person is suicidal but hasn't been caught making an attempt, he may still need someone with him until the crisis passes. Leave no weapons on the premises. That includes guns, knives, ropes, medication or any household cleaners that could be poisonous.

Where do you go for help in a suicidal crisis?

If the victim has already injured himself and is in a medical emergency, call an ambulance. He'll receive immediate care in the emergency room, but probably little attention will be given to psychological and emotional needs.

If the individual has not made an attempt but has shown signs he may be seriously depressed and could become self-destructive, there are several options.

The family physician. He could be the place to start. If necessary, the physician could give referrals. But be sure he doesn't pass a situation off as "a kid's trick" or give a two-week supply of pills and a pat on the shoulder.

Crisis centers. Many cities have walk-in centers where depressed youth and their parents can receive help. Go with them if necessary.

Hotlines. A depressed youth can call a hotline to talk with a trained interventionist. Counselors at crisis centers and hotlines may urge an individual to see a therapist.

Professional counselors. Get recommendations from those you trust. One psychotherapist told me, "Parents call me telling me that their adolescent is depressed but won't go to a counselor. I tell them to get him here, period, no matter how the teen protests. Then it's up to me."

Whatever professionals you consult — from family physician to therapist — be sure they are adequately trained to deal with the many facets of suicide intent. Locate a Christian psychologist or psychiatrist if at all possible. Their world view — so crucial in a problem that has spiritual roots — will be of great value.

Mental health or children's service agencies. They may be able to make recommendations of counselors or clinics and other resources available in your area.

Pastors. Ministers who are trained in counseling, who are sympathetic, who have an understanding of emotional problems, may be an option. Ask yourself whether their spiritual perspective is one that will help or hinder a teen who may feel guilty and angry.

You may make the contact with the counselor for the individual and go with him if he wants you to. But if you sense a teen needs it, do urge him to go for an evaluation. Since parents are the primary care persons, they should be notified when an adolescent seems to be displaying warning signs. But some will deny that their child could have a problem. If they do shrug off what you say, talk to your pastor or youth leader for advice. Together, work toward getting help for the teen if it seems necessary.

LONG-TERM HELP

The period when a depressed youth seems to be improving can be the most dangerous. Steve, for example, has been withdrawn. He slit his wrists and called someone right away to tell what he'd done. Now, though, he seems more like his old self — brighter, smiling more often.

Suicidologists warn that deeply depressed individuals have little emotional energy, but when they begin to feel better, perhaps because they've talked with someone about their suicidal feelings and then those feelings return, they do have the energy to act. Don't be fooled.

Some may resist your efforts to befriend them and all you can do is get help, pray and stand by their family. Even if they *are* hostile, keep assuring the youth that life can get better, that there is hope and that you are willing to be involved with them.

When it seems appropriate, assure young people considering suicide that God loves them. The fact that He loves them will seem incongruous to a teen who's been ignored, abused, denigrated and neglected — to whom life is an existential nightmare. Go slowly and use patient understanding.

Quietly let them know that you love them. Then show what God is like. Show Christ to them, taking into account that they may have had few positive relationships with adults before and may judge you by others who have hurt them. One counselor said that if a congregation overwhelms a troubled youth with loving concern, it may seem unreal to that young person. A wise assessment of the situation is crucial.

If God is leading you to do so, commit yourself to stay close. (Of course, always stay with them when suicide is an immediate threat, at least until help comes.) When I was depressed, one of the toughest things to handle was when someone promised to be my friend, then got sidetracked.

Keep turning their attention to alternatives to suicide. Some counselors ask the youth to sign a contract stating they will not kill themselves. Such contracts may seem pretty useless, but results hint that a commitment like that is helpful. One young person who made a contract stated it "removed a heavy burden."[5] There could be situations where suggesting the teen enter into such an agreement with you would be useful.

They'll need long-term friends. That may mean receiving phone calls at inopportune times. Emergencies in the middle of the night. Listening while the teen goes over and over the same thing. Investing the time you'd like for yourself. If the young person has been withdrawn and without social skills, it may take time to form a network of people who will work together to see the teen through. You may have an inordinate amount of involvement until that happens.

Help them get exercise. Find little things outside themselves on which they can focus: a burger with you in a quiet eatery, a trip to a ball game. Listen together to a tape of their favorite group. No high-decibel, high-energy parties. They're probably not ready for that yet.

Even our best efforts won't save every teen. But as Ann Spoonhour (whose son Justin committed suicide at fourteen, and who has been actively involved in suicide prevention since) says, "That doesn't mean that you shouldn't try to do something."[6]

It probably won't be a professional who first picks up the clues that a youth may be suicidal. It'll more likely be a parent, neighbor, teacher, Sunday school teacher, cousin, friend, youth worker, pastor, pewmate. So the layperson's part cannot be overestimated.

The American Association of Suicidology agrees, "The cardinal rule of suicide prevention is this: DO SOMETHING. If someone you know has attempted suicide and has not received professional care: GET HELP. If someone you know threatens to end his life: GET HELP. If someone you know has undergone a drastic change in his life and begins preparing wills or giving away personal possessions: GET HELP. Don't wait to see if other signs develop. Don't decide to consider it for a while. Do it today. Tomorrow may be too late."[7]

BRINGING IT HOME

Investigate resources for crisis intervention in your area. Hotlines? What helps are available through mental health agencies and children's service agencies? Does your church provide scholarships for teens who can't afford it but need counseling? Do you know a Christian counselor to whom you could refer a teen in trouble? If not, get some reliable resources.

With another person, or in a group, role play a conversation in which you take turns pretending to be a teen with suicidal thoughts who has given clues to his problem but is afraid to admit and talk about it. Follow the suggestions in this book to draw them out. Discuss what the next step should be.

16

NETWORKING TOGETHER

THE HAMILTONS' STORY

"Our daughter was fourteen when she started showing signs of depression. She cut herself off from her friends. She wasn't sleeping at night. My husband and I took turns napping and trying to talk to her — do anything to get her to sleep. But she wouldn't communicate with us and we couldn't tell what was going on inside her.

"Sandy always was more sensitive than my other children. She got a fraction of the spankings they did. All you had to do was talk sharply to her and she'd cry. She was the good child. Her brother was the one who required all the attention, because he was into things a lot more.

"We moved when she was about thirteen and she hated the new school. I've since learned that there was an educator in that school who may have paid more attention to the kids than he should have. But if anything happened, the trauma is so deep-seated Sandy has never talked about it.

"When she was four years old, Sandy received Jesus Christ into her life. We always took her to Sunday school and church, so Christianity was part of her life.

"It seemed to us that her depression came on suddenly — the withdrawal, the sleeplessness. I talked with her teachers and they said they noticed a change in her behavior, too. The school counselors tried to be nice, but they didn't seem to know how to cope. I know they have heavy caseloads. All the normal kids had a counselor. Maybe schools need one to take care of kids who have real problems.

"Teachers were concerned, too, but didn't know what to do to help. Maybe they need more training in that area.

"For the next several years, Sandy was in and out of hospitals. During one hospitalization, she refused to eat or drink a single thing. I'd ask her, 'Are you trying to kill yourself?' She'd deny it, saying that was ridiculous, and get very angry. She was completely tube-fed, including water. After three months, they got to the place where they ran daily tests on her because her bodily functions were shutting down little by little. They told me that if something didn't happen, she wouldn't survive.

"She looked like death warmed over, like a skeleton with skin stretched over it. It was when she was so physically deteriorated that she had a seizure.

"I call that God's shock treatment. It was the only one she ever had, but it scared her. She thought she was going to die. That's a paradox, because that's what she was trying to do — kill herself. She felt that by not eating, she was taking control of her life. Now the control was taken away by the seizure.

"She started eating again. But she was a long way from being well. (After she got well, she admitted to me that she had been trying to kill herself.) The hospital thought that her 'religious paraphernalia' (her Bible, Christian books and music tapes) were detrimental to her recovery. They took it all away from her. We became unglued and fought for it.

"Then they decided to use Sandy's 'religious paraphernalia' as a reward. If she did what she was supposed to, she'd be able to use them. If not, it would be taken away.

"Counseling had come to a standstill because the psychiatrist said Sandy could talk in their sessions about anything except religion. As far as Sandy was concerned, though, if they wouldn't let her talk about what was on her mind, she wouldn't talk about anything at all.

"She hadn't been taking her medication, either. Finally, she told the staff that she hadn't taken it in three weeks and since she didn't intend to take it when she was released, she requested they take her off it so they could document what happened when they did. They went along with her.

"She proved to them that she did fine without the medication and was soon released. She's been out of the hospital for four years and has had no regression.

"There were people who helped her so much. One of her friends from church stuck by her all through her illness. Sandy didn't even act as though she cared that the friend was there, but Marlene seemed to understand that Sandy wasn't reacting normally and kept coming back. Many people didn't know how to deal with her, though, and tended to shy away. A lot of her peers weren't sure how to relate to her. Maybe kids should be made more aware so they know how to relate.

"My brother, a minister, visited Sandy regularly, too. It was frustrating for him, because Sandy often talked about the same things over and over. But he tried to be patient. It helped that they had a good relationship before Sandy got sick.

"Some of the youth leaders from church stuck by her, too. During periods when Sandy was out of the hospital, they took her on youth retreats, and assured me they'd watch out for her. And they did.

"The staff who made the most impact on her and who got closest to her were the ones who gave her unconditional love. Whether or not she wanted it, she got a big bear hug. She knew they accepted her, even if she acted in strange ways.

"They spent time with her, just let her talk, and tried to be her friend. They'd take her for a Coke and if she wanted to talk, fine. If not, fine, too. They never put Sandy under pressure to perform. She was already under internal pressure that none of us can understand. There was a torment going on inside her.

"Others tried to relate, but when she started acting oddly, they backed off. I could understand, so I couldn't be upset with them. It was a new experience for all of us.

"Kids like Sandy need people around them who'll let them know they're loved. Who'll take the initiative. Sandy was withdrawn. She wouldn't seek anyone's help. When all this began, people would try to say 'hello' or talk to her in church and she'd just mumble. One woman tried and tried to engage her in conversation and Sandy would only mumble a greeting.

"Recently, Sandy told me she was going to this woman's house on an errand. It seems Sandy had initiated a conversation with this woman at church recently. The woman told me it was the first time Sandy had ever done that. The reason it happened was because this woman had persisted in befriending Sandy even though my daughter wasn't responsive.

"Touching and hugging is important. When I touched her, she'd become tense all through her body. I decided to hug anyway, and there were times when I could feel the tension relaxing a little. I decided: *I'm not going to give in to this. This girl of mine is going to know that I love her.* The church staff who were able to keep a relationship with her through her illness were ones who did just that.

"It's hard to know how to deal with a child who is going through this kind of illness. You feel as though everything you try to do is the wrong thing. I told a doctor that — that I felt as though I was doing everything wrong. He told me, 'You're not. You're doing everything that a parent in the same situation would do.' "

NETWORKING DEMONSTRATED

Sandy's parents *did* care and did all they could for her. But suppose no one had been tuned in to Sandy's depression. Suppose her parents had shrugged and turned away. "Don't be silly. What have you got to be miserable about? You're only a kid!" Considering Sandy's depressed condition and her severe self-destructive tendencies, she could easily be dead now.

Her parents weren't the only ones who contributed to her recovery. Notice the others who networked together:

Extended family.
Teachers.
School counselors.
Church workers.
Helping professionals.
Peers.
Church members.
Of these, except for helping professionals, many felt

inadequate. Her parents had never gone through anything like this before and imagined they were doing everything wrong. Her uncle became discouraged when Sandy kept going back to issues he thought had been resolved. Teachers and counselors were sympathetic but seemed not to have sufficient time or training to help. Some peers, church workers and church members who could have provided support hung back because Sandy's behavior frightened them away or her unresponsiveness fooled them into thinking they weren't wanted or needed.

The survival of the Sandys we know can depend to a significant degree on whether we are trained in prevention and intervention and are willing to embrace the Samaritan principle — networking as God calls us to do.

SEEING IS BELIEVING

Our youth's survival depends, too, on whether we are willing to model Christ, especially when the people who are supposed to teach them love and trust fail. Like Lenore, who's father sexually abused her when she was a young teen. Her mother knew, but failed to stop him. And when Lenore reported it to the police and he was jailed, she was blamed for doing so.[1]

We *all* need heroes, but youth need them most. And what they have are not heroes, but celebrities. Bigger-than-life, widely-publicized musclemen who decimate their enemy with a spray of bullets and a roar. Sweating rock stars who pound the air with their beat.

"Here you are, trying to figure out what life is all about — who in the world you are. How to be a person people will notice, how to be different from the rest of your family, maybe," one young man only recently through his teens told me.

Along come celebrities — the lauded and applauded — throwing kisses to their groupies and disappearing in sleek limos. *Dress like them. Wear their names on t-shirts.* If these idols make adults groan and cringe, that's fine, too.

Why no more heroes? Because this is the era of the exposé. Set heroes up and see them knocked down like milk bottles at a carnival.

So cynicism comes early. Presidents have feet of clay, youth have discovered. And professional athletes, too. In 1986, All-American basketball star Len Bias died from cocaine intoxication while celebrating his selection by the Boston Celtics in the NBA draft. A week later, toxicologists confirmed that cocaine killed Cleveland Browns football star Don Rogers the day before he was to be married.

More disillusionment for youth. Originally, a hero was "a man of great strength and courage, favored by the gods and in part descended from them, often regarded as a half-god and worshiped after his death."[2] The word came to mean a person admired for his courage, qualities and achievements and regarded as a model.

"A classical hero is supposed to enlarge our possibilities," writes Pete Axthelm.[3] But he must be able to stand the scrutiny. That's a tough order. No one can be courageous and beneficent all the time.

Only the God-man can do that. So we tell teens, "Don't look at me. Look at Jesus."

Commendable. But youth need flesh and blood heroes, too — humans like themselves in whom they can see the God-man is incarnate. Ones who sin, who confess quickly and who have learned to say, "I'm sorry." Role models whose lives are inspiring but attainable.

So here we are, back in the spotlight.

We can't get away from it. *We are called to be heroes.* Not the larger-than-life, John-Wayne, "Head-'em-off-at-the-pass" kind. Human beings in whom the God-man lives *now,* people crucified with Christ but alive and living by faith in the Son of God. Like the ones in the Hebrews Hall of Fame: "Gideon, Barak, Samson, Jephthah, David, Samuel and the prophets, who through faith conquered kingdoms, administered justice, and gained what was promised; who shut the mouth of lions, quenched the fury of the flames, and escaped the edge of the sword; whose weakness was turned to strength; and who became powerful in battle and routed foreign armies" (Hebrews 11:32-34).

"Bill Russell once said that kids should be dissuaded from idolizing athletes. Better, he said, to focus on the good people closest to them — whether they be parents or teachers or religious leaders.

"Here is everyday, intimate contact, and not some commercialized, hyperbolized, superficial, view of man or woman."[4]

Youth need heroes, and the heroes they need are us.

So pray for yourself. Pray for teens. Pray with them. Pray that God will lead you to the young person in your particular world who is severely depressed. He wants to help us get to them in time. So we won't sit weeping at a funeral like my youth leader friend, asking ourselves:

"Why didn't I know?"

BRINGING IT HOME

Think of yourself as a potential member of a network in the life of a teen you know. Think of a teen in each of the categories (parent, extended family, neighbor, etc.). What is your role with each and how can you function more effectively?

Study Hebrews 11. Ask God to show you specific ways you can become a better role model for teens you know. Translate those things into practical terms (*e.g.*, faith to worry less so I won't be so preoccupied and will be more friendly to the teenager next door).

Make a list of youth you know with specific needs. Pray regularly for them. Ask God to give you an opportunity to build a relationship with one of them. Then, take the initiative whenever *He* gives the opportunity.

Things Teens Need to Know

- A desire to kill yourself is only temporary. The thoughts that bring about that desire can be changed. *You can be helped.*

- You may only mean to scare people by cutting yourself a little so they'll pay attention to you. But you could make a mistake and kill yourself or cripple yourself for life.

- Everyone has problems — even Christians.

- Hurting yourself is no way to solve problems. There are people who want to help you when you're desperate. If you're preoccupied with thoughts of death or of hurting yourself, contact your parents, another family member, a pastor, a youth leader. Or call a crisis hotline.

- Everyone feels angry and discouraged sometimes. But those feelings don't have to control you; with help, you can learn to control them.

- If someone you know is desperate and is thinking of hurting himself, *get help fast.*

- Your life does *not* belong to you. It belongs to God. You do not have the right to take it.

- You may feel all alone in the universe, as though no one loves you. That's not true. The most powerful person of all loves you — God Almighty, creator of heaven and earth.

- No matter what you may think, you *are* an important person. Talented. God has a purpose in mind for your life and He wants to show you what it is.

● No life is so messed up that God can't step in and make it work.

● Those who are supposed to love you may not do so. They may inflict pain on you instead. That doesn't mean there's something wrong with you. They do it because they have a sinful nature. Sin and Satan are the reason the world is so messed up.

● We all have a sinful nature — even you. But Christ died to pay for our sins. To receive forgiveness, we must tell God we know we are sinners and ask Jesus Christ to come into our lives. He will.

● God will forgive every one of your sins and you can start over. He'll help you overcome sin a little at time. If you mess up again, He'll forgive you because He loves you. Because you love Him, you won't want to take advantage of His mercy.

● People will not always understand you. They will not always be there for you. They can't. They're human like you.

● God is the only friend who understands you completely and whose love never changes no matter what. If you've accepted Christ, He lives in you. He wants to be close to you and you to Him and to lead you through all the hard places every day.

● You need to be part of a group of Christians who love one another, are honest with one another and help one another any way they can. That's one way God will show His love for you.

● It's OK to ask for help when you need it. Go to a mature family member, friend, pastor or other church staff member, or a counselor with whom you feel at home.

Things Adults Need to Know

- Since between 500,000 and two million youth make suicide attempts every year, it's reasonable to suppose one of them may be present in your world at some time. He or she may need you to help cope.

- A desire to kill oneself is a clue that the individual has a distorted perception of what life and death are all about.

- Christians are called to be life-savers. We cannot, with good conscience, limit that to evangelistic invitations in Sunday school class and in church meetings. Suicide prevention and intervention are lifesaving, too.

- We cannot, with a wave of a wand, produce a stress-free environment for youth. We *do* need to do all we can to attack the primary external factors that cause debilitating stress. Work *against* violence, *for* peace; *against* child abuse, *for* strong families. Knowing that these are the last days and that things will get worse is not an excuse for lethargy.

- To help youth, we must understand something about who they are, why they act the way they do and what they want and need. That takes work.

- From sermons, Sunday school lessons and personal testimonies, church-going youth learn the basic facts about Christ. But unless they experience Him in their relationships with us as well, facts won't make a whole lot of difference.

- Every Christian can help build a healthy sense of esteem into youth they know. Don't just leave the job up to parents.

- It's *right* to be involved in your church program. It's *wrong* to be so involved in committees and planning sessions that you have no time for the needy kid God keeps bringing into your life.

- Ideas to update Christian education, youth ministries and other youth related activities do not have to originate only with the church staff. Others can make suggestions. Are you on the lookout for creative ways to reach troubled youth? Are you willing to help implement them? The suggestion to introduce suicide prevention and intervention programs in your church can come from you, too.

- The kids who need help most may be cynical, foul-mouthed aberrations. See what's beyond the leather and chains; listen in order to hear what's behind the four-letter words.

- Christians who shrug off the educational system as sold out to secularism and spend most of their time moaning, "Ain't it awful!" instead of doing something about it, no matter how small, are selling out their youth.

- With all the stress on how to be a success, we may have forgotten to teach youth how to deal with failure. They will goof, but that doesn't mean they *are* failures.

- Youth need us to help them discover their gifts and to provide opportunities for them to cultivate and use those gifts.

- Is communication with your teenager poor? Let appropriate members of your church staff, educational leaders and other key people know that you want to work with them in helping to improve it.

- Above all, adults need to know what they believe. What is your life philosophy? In what ways are you communicating a Christian world view to youth? In what areas do you need to improve?

Resources

FILM

The Question, directed by Fred Carpenter, Mars Hill Production (NR). Available for rental from Youth for Christ. Discussion guide available.

BOOKS

A Reason For Hope: When Your Child is on Drugs or Alcohol, Andre Bustanoby, Here's Life Publishers, 1986.
Crisis Counseling, H. Norman Wright, Here's Life Publishers, 1985.
Christian Counseling, Gary R. Collins, Ph.D., Word Books, 1980.
A Cry for Help, Mary Griffin and Carol Elsenthel, Doubleday and Co., 1981.
Growing Up Dead, Brenda Rabkin, Abington, 1978.
Too Young to Die: Youth and Suicide, Francine Klagsbrun, Houghton Mifflin Co., 1976.
Suicide — Prevention, Intervention, Postvention, Earl A. Grollman, Beacon Hill Press, 1971.
The Suicidal Patient, Recognition, Intervention, Management, Victor M. Victoroff, M.D., Medical Economics Press, 1983.
Depression and Its Treatment, John H. Griest, M.D. and James W. Jefferson, M.D., American Psychiatric Press, Inc., 1984.
Coping with Teenage Depression, Kathleen McCoy, New American Library, 1982.

SUICIDE PREVENTION AND INTERVENTION ORGANIZATIONS

CONTACT Teleministries, USA, Inc., Pouch A., Harrisburg, PA 17105. Information available on opening a CONTACT center. Also a list of CONTACT centers.

The American Association of Suicidology, 2459 S.
Ash, Denver, Co. 80222. Educational pamphlets
available and guidelines for groups interested in
beginning crisis facilities.

The Samaritans, 500 Commonwealth Ave., Kenmore
Square, Boston, MA 02215. Educational material
available.

Suicide Prevention and Crisis Center of San Mateo
County, 1811 Trousdale Dr., Burlingame, Ca. 94010.
Educational material available.

National Institute of Mental Health, 5600 Fishers
Lane, Rockville, Maryland 20857. Public Inquiries
Branch, Rm. 15C-05. Information on suicide and
related subjects available.

CRISIS CENTERS

They may be listed in your phone book under
"Suicide," "Crisis," "Mental Health," or
"Counseling." Also consult the front of your phone
book for a listing of local crisis centers. Look in
the white pages to see if a center associated with
CONTACT or The Samaritans is located in your
area. In an emergency if you find no resource
immediately available, call the police or your local
emergency number. In a medical emergency, call an
ambulance.

Notes

Chapter One
1. The Samaritans, "Depression, Suicide and the College Student."
2. "These Teenagers Feel That They Have No Options," *People*, February 18, 1985.
3. George Howe Colt, "Suicide in America," *Reader's Digest*, January, 1984, p. 99.
4. Scott Kraft, "Mom . . . I Was Never OK," *Statesman-Journal*, Salem, OR, March 23, 1983.

Chapter Two
1. Tom Gorman, "'Values' surveys ensnarl public schools in privacy concerns," *The Oregonian*, Portland, OR, July 28, 1985.
2. James W. Sire, *The Universe Next Door*, (Downer's Grove, IL: InterVarsity Press, 1976), p. 101.
3. As quoted by Kandy Stroud, "Stop Pornographic Rock," *Newsweek*, May 6, 1985, p. 14.
4. "Joined in life, death," *Statesman-Journal*, Salem, OR, pp. 7, 28, 86.
5. Edwin Newman, *Strictly Speaking*, (New York: The Bobbs-Merril Co., Inc., 1974), p. 11.
6. Steven Stack, "A Leveling Off in Young Suicides," *The Wall Street Journal*, May 28, 1986.
7. "Right Now," *McCalls*, October, 1981, p. 46.
8. Randy C. Alcorn, *Christians in the Wake of the Sexual Revolution* (Portland, OR: Multnomah Press, 1985), p. 63.
9. "Right Now," *McCalls*, October, 1981, p. 46.

Chapter Three
1. Luella Cole and Irma Nelson Hall, *Psychology of Adolescence*, 6th Edition (New York: Holt, Rinehart and Winston, Inc., 1965), p.3.
2. Bruce Narramore, *Adolescence is Not an Illness* (Old Tappan, NJ: Fleming H. Revell, 1980), p. 29.
3. Cole and Hall, *Psychology of Adolescence* pp. 240, 241.

Chapter Four
1. John H. Griest, M.D., & James W. Jefferson, M.D., *Depression and Its Treatment,* (Washington, D.C.: American Psychiatric Press, 1984), p.32.
2. Griest, p.1.
3. Francine Klagsbrun, *Too Young to Die* (Boston, MA: Houghton Mifflin Co., 1976), p. 35.
4. "No Other Out," *The Banner,* October 13, 1986, pp. 10-11.
5. Kathleen McCoy, *Coping with Teenage Depression* (New York: New American Library, 1982), p.12.
6. Gary R. Collins, Ph.D., *Christian Counseling* (Waco, TX: Word Books, 1980), p.86.
7. Bill Nagler, M.D., and Janet-Prunier-Steffens, R.N., "Teenage Suicide," *Let's Live,* December, 1984, p.14.
8. Gary R. Collins, Ph.D., *Christian Counseling* (Waco, TX: Word Books, 1980), p. 87.
9. Emery Nester, *Depression* (Portland, OR: Multnomah Press, 1983), p.179.

Chapter Five
1. Webster's New World Dictionary.
2. Hal Lindsey, with C.C. Carlson, *The Terminal Generation* (New York: Bantam Books, 1976), p. 99.
3. Kenneth S. Wuest, *Wuest's Word Studies,* Vol. 3 (Grand Rapids, MI: Wm. B. Eerdman's Publishing Co., 1969), p.21.

Chapter Six
1. McCandish Phillips, "War on the Young," *Alliance Witness,* February 13, 1974, pp.24, 26.

Chapter Seven
1. Dorothy Edwards Shuttlesworth, *Exploring Nature With Your Child* (New York: Greystone Press, 1952), p. 17.
2. Hal Lindsey, with C.C. Carlson, *The Terminal Generation* (New York: Bantam Books, 1976), p.111.
3. Leontine Young, *The Fractured Family* (New York: McGraw Hill Book Co., 1973).

Chapter Eight
1. Luella Cole and Irma Nelson Hall, *Psychology of Adolescence* (New York: Holt, Rinehart and Winston, Inc., 1965), p.269.